Winning Words:
A New Approach to Developing Effective Speaking Skills

The Mitterling Method:
Carol Coulter
Ann Duke
Machelle Curtis
Kim Mitterling

CBI

CBI Publishing Company, Inc.
51 Sleeper Street
Boston, Massachusetts 02210

Production Editor: Donna L. Miner
Interior Designer: TKM Productions
Cover Designer: MaryEllen Podgorski
Illustrator: Monica Queenan
Compositor: TKM Productions

Library of Congress Cataloging in Publication Data
Main entry under title:

Winning words, a new approach to developing
    effective speaking skills.

    Bibliography: p. 177.
    1. Public speaking. I. Duke, Ann.
II. Title: Mitterling method.
PN4121.W47   808.5′1   81-38491
ISBN 0-8436-0869-2   AACR2

Printed in the United States of America

CONTENTS

ACKNOWLEDGMENTS:

The successful completion of any book requires the pooling of many resources. The ideas generated and expressed in the following pages are no exception. A team of four authors contributed to the written content. We are also indebted to the past participants of thousands of seminars held across the country. Without their combined experiences our efforts could not have produced the stories and examples from which you will learn.

We also extend our thanks to Stan Galek and Donna Miner for assisting us in the editing process. Their comments and careful review added the finishing touches that are a necessary part of any final product.

Finally, we would like to express our special thanks to Robert N. Anderson, the Chief Executive Officer of The Mitterling Method. His inquiries of ''When will you finish?'' provided the encouragement needed to meet numerous deadlines. In addition, the title *Winning Words* is the result of his creativity.

Meet Bob Emerson, the everyman of the executive world. Moderately successful, Bob has been climbing his way up the corporate ladder for seventeen years. A closer look would result in the following composite:

Name: Robert A. Emerson
Occupation: Assistant Vice-President of Marketing at Watson, Inc. for the past ten years
Previous Employment: Account Executive for Merrimack Metal Corporation for seven years
Education: B.A. in Business Administration from State University
Technical Courses in engineering through a continuing education program
Age: 38
Height: 6 ft.
Weight: 195 lbs.
Marital Status: Married, with two children

Recently Bob was given a rare opportunity. His boss, Mr. Watson, turned over to Bob an invitation to speak at a technicians' conference to introduce Watson's new product line of computerized machinery. Mr. Watson had always preferred to save these engagements for himself; he had never felt anyone could do as good a job. However, this time, he was scheduled to be out of town at an important management meeting, so the task fell to Bob.

When Bob met with Mr. Watson to receive all the pertinent data regarding the upcoming conference, the meeting ended with, "Bob, I'm sure I don't need to emphasize the importance of this presentation to you. I *know* you won't disappoint me."

Translation—"Don't mess this one up, or you're in big trouble." Registering the unspoken message, Bob sets out to meet the challenge.

Bob feels apprehensive. Although this is a great opportunity, he has always felt unsure of his ability to present his ideas formally before large groups of people. Meetings of ten to twenty people rarely cause him any anxiety. In his position as assistant vice-president of marketing, Bob's responsibilities include presenting a weekly report to the directors of his department, the production department, and numerous colleagues. Bob likes to feel in control. In meeting environments he responds well to questions and comments, and feels he is able to keep the meeting on track. In interpersonal situations as well, he is confident that he will convey a dynamic, accurate message.

Formal presentations, however, are another matter. Bob can never understand the major changes that occur in the short walk from the chair to the podium. In that small span of time his confident, controlled demeanor fades to a lackluster, uncertain appearance.

Bob is acutely aware of this Dr. Jekyll/Mr. Hyde transformation. He has made serious attempts in the past to improve his speaking skills. He recently attended a series of lectures on public speaking. One element that impressed him was the use of humor as an introductory vehicle. Bob thinks that humor will help him to relax while entertaining his audience at the same time. He has always felt that a public speaker should be an entertainer. The other concept Bob took to heart was that of practice. He had always left the preparation of other presentations to the last minute. This time he vows he'll make sure he has the proper rehearsal.

Bob's feeling of comfort regarding the upcoming conference increases as he considers his in-depth knowledge of the new product. After all, he was instrumental in researching and developing all the marketing strategies. There's no one at Watson, Inc. that understands all the features and benefits of the new machinery line better than he does. Finally, Bob realizes that Mr. Watson would not have entrusted the assignment to him if he was not the most logical choice to get the job done.

The following Wednesday, two days before the scheduled presentation, Bob figures he had best set out a plan of attack. That evening over a cup of coffee the timetable unfolds. Bob figures that tonight he will organize his thoughts, and on Thursday he will practice, leaving Friday morning for a final review before the conference.

Thursday night's practice reveals several rough spots. But as he continues to rehearse he feels increasingly confident of polishing his delivery. During the past week he tried his introductory joke on several associates with unanimous success. As Bob stands before his bathroom mirror and delivers the punchline one last time, he knows that this time he will succeed.

Friday morning dawns, and Bob pulls out his favorite three-piece navy blue suit. "May as well look the part of the successful executive," he thinks, as he gets dressed. At the office he has his usual three cups of coffee, then closets himself in the office to finish reviewing his materials. Twelve o'clock arrives. Bob pulls all of his papers together, places them in his briefcase, takes one last look around the office to make sure nothing has been forgotten, and heads for the conference.

Bob walks into the main conference room, and although the sight of all those chairs makes him a bit nervous, he is certain that once he begins speaking, everything will be fine. At 1:30, conference participants begin to filter in from lunch. There is an air of camaraderie reflected in their laughter, conversation and dress. In fact, Bob speculates, their attire could almost pass for a uniform. All stroll by casually dressed: in shirts whose pockets are stuffed with pens, rumpled corduroy slacks or skirts, and tweed jackets thrown over their shoulders. Each tie even has the same look—slightly askew. Bob's thoughts turn to his original purpose in scanning the crowd—to find the coordinator and learn his spot on the agenda. He finds her and learns he won't be speaking until 4:00 p.m. The last presenter. "Terrific," Bob thinks, "I'll have more time to review my thoughts."

At 1:45 p.m. Bob finds a spot close to the podium so that when his turn comes to speak he won't have far to walk. He turns to look back at the crowd that is still moving in from lunch. His chest tightens, and he suddenly notices beads of perspiration forming on his upper lip and forehead. "God, it's getting awfully warm in here. I'll be glad when this is over and I can leave."

At 2:00 p.m. the first speaker begins what is to be an hour–long monologue on the methods of increasing productivity. Bob hears the clearing of throats and the shifting of tired bodies as the speaker at long last draws his presentation to a close.

Next on the agenda is a slide show on a product that is being introduced by another company. "At least they're not a competitor" is all Bob can think of as he wipes his brow for the third time. When the slide show is almost finished, Bob feels genuine panic setting in. His heart sounds as if at any moment it will jump out of his chest, and breathing is increasingly difficult, if not impossible.

4:00 p.m.: Bob's mind turns blank as he hears "Ladies and gentlemen, please give a warm welcome to the representative from Watson, Inc.—Mr. Robert Emerson." Somehow Bob finds his way to the podium. "Thank you." The microphone whines, and Bob jumps back and tries again. "Uh . . . thank you, Mr. Moderator, for that fine introduction. I am delighted to be here." Bob clears his throat as his mind grasps for the beginning phrase of his opening joke. "You see this is, well, a fine opportunity for me to let you know about our new product line." Bob looks up into a sea of faces, then back down, frantically searching for a word, any word, to get him started on the right track. In his haze of fear, he focuses on the first phrase of the presentation, grips the podium and begins, "There's an old story about . . ." As Bob recites the joke that seemed so hysterically funny last night, he experiences the familiar sinking sensation he had hoped to conquer. He realizes that, once again, he is dying.

The story completed, a few polite chuckles echo through the room. The audience shifts. A few whispers can be heard from the back of the room as Bob clears his throat to continue. "Well, as I said before, my purpose in being here is to introduce our dynamic new product. But to really appreciate the features of the new line, we should review the historical evolution of this type of machinery. Next we need to look at the old machine's capabilities and limitations. Then I'll explain the new technology that has led to the computerized equipment and how that new technology overcomes the limitations we have experienced to date. Finally, I'll review a few of the future enhancements you can look forward to acquiring in the up-and-coming months." The next half hour is interrupted by an occasional cough and the shuffle of feet as a few audience members exit. Throughout, Bob is oblivious. Getting his information out and sitting down are now his only objectives. At long last, he sees he is at the end of his presentation. "And that, ladies and gentlemen, is the whole Watson story." Dick clears his throat for what seems like the hundredth time and weakly asks, "Are there any questions?" The answer returns in the form of a less than enthusiastic round of applause. He turns with a sigh of relief, heads blindly to his chair, and collapses in exhaustion.

Oblivious to the mass exodus to the bar, Bob sits in a depressed stupor, reliving his recent fiasco. Even the entrance of maintenance men to clean and set up for the next day's meetings has no effect.

"Sir . . . excuse me . . . sir . . . you'll have to leave now. We need to lock this room for tomorrow."

Bob blinks once, then twice. Staring blankly at the young man, he stands and turns to leave. Suddenly from the corner of the darkened conference room, a voice booms out—

Ⓦ "Bob, Bob Emerson!"

Bob looks around in confusion, searching for the maintenance man that was standing next to him only seconds ago.

BE: "What is this, some kind of joke?" Bob mutters to the seemingly deserted room.

The voice booms again, now so loud that it echoes through the empty space.

Ⓦ "This is no joke, Bob. My name is Wonder Word, and I am here to talk to you about the presentation you made today."

BE: Bob sighs to himself, "I shouldn't let these presentations rattle me this way. After all, I didn't perform that badly. I can't imagine why I would be upset enough to hallucinate. Of course, the last time I gave a speech I felt extremely light–headed. Maybe I should see a doctor."

Ⓦ "Bob, you don't need to see a doctor. You need to see me. I have been observing you for many years, and your recurring problem troubles me. You're a credible, successful businessman, but you never portray that image in a formal presentation."

BE: "Look Mr. Word, or whoever you are, I don't need any reminders from my own hallucination regarding my poor performances. Believe me, if I could erase everything that's happened behind a podium in the past, I would." Bob stops, shakes his head in disbelief—"This is astounding; now I'm talking to myself. I need to go home and get some rest."

Ⓦ "Bob, you are not imagining anything. I am Wonder Word, and I'm here to help you become an effective speaker."

BE: Bob laughs as he replies, "Is that right? Well, you'd better find someone with potential."

Ⓦ   "You need help!" Wonder Word thunders. "and I've decided to take your case whether you like it or not."

BE: "What do you mean *my case*?" Bob asks with increasing interest.

Ⓦ   "I can't stand to see you suffer any longer. (Not to mention your audiences.) I'm going to give you something—*a second chance*."

BE: "What do you mean, a second chance? After this last presentation, I've decided to give up all speaking engagements."

Ⓦ   "If I could help you achieve your goal of being a successful presenter, would you reconsider?"

BE: "Sure, but I've tried everything."

Ⓦ   "This is going to be tougher than I thought. Why do you think they call me Wonder Word? I can teach you all of the elements you need to make your presentations effective. Then, when you've acquired the skills you need, you can be sent back in time to your technicians' conference. You'll be able to give your presentation the right way. My way."

BE: "Forgive my skepticism, Wonder Word, but I just wasn't cut out to be a public speaker . . . still, I've never been one to pass up an opportunity, especially when it comes to business." Bob sits down, dazed by the strange, enticing prospect.

Ⓦ   "Well, Bob, are you interested? Because if not, there's a lady in L.A. who will be needing my help very soon."

BE: "Wait, Wonder Word, don't leave. Yes, I'm interested. I do need your help. Where do we begin?"

Ⓦ   "You have begun, Bob. You've admitted that you need my help."

"Wonder Word? You must be kidding!" our publisher said when we presented him with our initial manuscript. But after further reading he discovered our purpose in creating a fictional character.

Although you won't find Wonder Word in *Larousse's World Mythology,* he fulfills a very important role. There's no single image that readers can relate to as the ideal presenter. Because the ideal varies from group to group, only an imaginary being could be right all of the time. Wonder Word is the ultimate role model from which to learn.

In our experience, people learn best when they can participate. Thus, we use the conversational mode to facilitate a discussion reflecting your questions and thoughts. The questions Bob poses are ones we've heard in numerous seminars from a variety of individuals. They represent the major concerns professionals have regarding public speaking.

Bob felt as if he'd lost whenever he presented. A loss of self-control caused a loss of audience interest and ultimately, he lost self-esteem. Perhaps your experiences have never been as extreme, but every presenter loses when the image he projects falls short of his objectives. And Wonder Word can help there, too.

The purpose of this book is to improve *your* presentational skills regardless of your previous experience. Anyone, from beginners to experienced professionals, will benefit. The book begins with a needs analysis that allows each individual to assess his or her current delivery skills. Based on your own level of skill development, you can refer to some or all of the succeeding chapters for the appropriate information. Each chapter has worksheets to assist you in building your skills. Assignments are given that require use of the techniques provided. A final evaluation measures the changes that will occur.

If you haven't guessed by now, this is *not* another in the series of ''You can do it—if you think about it long enough'' books. It is, instead, a working guide for improving your public speaking skills. The book will work, but only if *you* do. To help you do this, we have produced a cassette that will review the ideas you'll find in *Winning Words*. The cassette discusses Wonder Word's techniques and tips, and also gives you the chance to *hear* examples of effective and ineffective speaking.

No one ever became a better presenter by reading about it.* You become better only by taking the chance, standing up before a group—any group—and presenting your ideas. So we, the authors, leave you with a challenge. Don't agree with everything Wonder Word professes. Question his authority as Bob will question it. Review his ideas with the cassette. But don't stop there—try the techniques for yourself. Because only by seeing them work will you truly believe in them. The winning results will be well worth the time you invest.

*The *Winning Words* cassette is available from the publisher of the book. A convenient order form can be found on the last page of *Winning Words*.

CHAPTER ONE

ARE YOU NORMAL?

One hundred sets of eyes are staring up at you, waiting for your words of wisdom, waiting to be entertained. This is your big moment to dazzle the audience with your wit. You can hear the sound of applause as you deliver your final statement. You imagine the compliments you'll receive on your excellent presentation.

Quickly you return to reality, and discover that you're actually flipping through the pages of your written speech, grasping for your thoughts, displaying signs of nervousness and sputtering forth a garbled message. Your experience has not turned out as you imagined.

Bob Emerson, our aspiring speaker, encountered such difficulties. Prior to his presentation he believed he would be successful. Yet he soon discovered that he lacked the confidence, control and skill necessary for success. During both the preparation and the delivery stages of his speech he tripped over some of the commonly experienced stumbling blocks to public speaking.

Bob Emerson is normal.

Several of Bob's stumbling blocks contained elements of fear. Fear of boring the audience, fear of standing up before the group, and fear of not remembering his thoughts. According to the *Book of Lists* by Irving Wallace, the #1 fear is *public speaking*, so Bob is not alone. His fears are further documented by the hundreds of participants who have taken our Presentation Skills Seminar. In addition to identifying with all of the stumbling blocks that Bob encountered, the experiences of these people further verify that these barriers can be overcome.

In this first chapter you, too, will have an opportunity to identify your stumbling blocks to public speaking. Then you will proceed, along with Bob, in analyzing past experiences and setting objectives. Subsequent chapters provide techniques which will assist you in eliminating, counteracting, or controlling your stumbling blocks.

The first step is to conduct a needs analysis, and then develop listening skills. Techniques to control nervousness and identify your communication style are provided. Methods for analyzing your audience, and appropriate use of interest elements, speech development and organization, and visual aids are discussed to help you further enhance your presentation skills. Information on specific situations such as question and answer sessions is included; this information will apply to certain types of presentational environments. Finally, the chapter entitled ''Ready, Set, Go'' provides the polishing touches and techniques for skill maintenance.

Throughout the book, Bob will learn presentation techniques from Wonder Word, our communication authority. Through his experience you will learn and grow as well. His questions and thoughts may reflect your own. So join with him to discover all the techniques that Wonder Word has to share.

Ⓦ   All right, Bob, let's begin at the beginning.

BE: There's so much I need to learn, I have no idea where the beginning is.

Ⓦ   That's why I'm here.

BE: And believe me, I'm thankful for that. Where do we start?

Ⓦ   Let's analyze your experience. How did you feel delivering your presentation? What specifically occurred?

BE: I was *bad.*

Ⓦ   Besides that, Bob, what,—let's say—*environmental* factors existed?

BE: Well, it was the end of the day, and everyone was tired.

Ⓦ   Good—audience tired. How did that make you feel?

BE: Scared me to death. I mean, before my turn to speak there was an excellent slide show, and all I had were notes and a joke.

Ⓦ   So you were nervous.

BE: So who isn't?

Ⓦ   Most everyone experiences some type of anxiety before they speak. How did your anxiety affect you?

BE: Well, I, I rushed through my entire script—read as fast as I could. I mean, I heard people moving around, some actually left, and I didn't want to take up much more of their time.

Ⓦ   Was your information important to you?

BE: Of course—it's my job.

Ⓦ   Was the information important to your audience?

BE: I would think so—they need our products.

Ⓦ   So your message *was* important to them.

BE: I really don't see what you're getting at, Wonder Word.

Ⓦ   You shouldn't have felt as though you were taking up their time. Your information applied to them, but how it was presented didn't interest them.

BE: I must say I can't blame them.

Ⓦ   So you were *nervous* and therefore *lost control* of the situation, and rapidly read your script.

BE: Exactly. I never can seem to maintain control in a presentation before a large group. Maybe you should abandon my case, Wonder Word.

Ⓦ   Let's not get carried away, Bob. You *were* bad, but you can learn from this experience to make the next one more positive. Why don't we look back and discover what else occurred.

BE: Well, when they didn't laugh at my joke, I felt like the audience was against me.

Ⓦ   All right—*fear* that the audience was judging you.

BE: That is precisely how I felt. I read the speech and I felt as though there was a wall between the audience and me. I don't even remember looking at anyone.

Ⓦ   Lack of rapport with the audience was a significant barrier for you, Bob. You've already identified several personal stumbling blocks. Take a look at the following list to discover any other feelings you may have experienced.

Stumbling Blocks Checklist

The following is a checklist of the common stumbling blocks that Wonder Word had Bob fill out.

Bob put a check in the column that best described how frequently his stumbling blocks occur. For those blocks that never occur, Bob has left the column blank.

STUMBLING BLOCKS	Seldom Occurs	Frequently Occurs	Always Occurs
1. Fear of not knowing the audience's predisposition toward you or your message.			
2. Lack of self-confidence			After ✓ performance
3. Feeling of over-confidence		Before ✓ performance	
4. Nervousness			✓
5. Loss of control		✓	
6. Inability to be conversational			✓
7. Fear of not having enough data to support your points	✓		
8. Feeling that you have to use exact language, and fearing that you will not be able to find a word			

STUMBLING BLOCKS	Seldom Occurs	Frequently Occurs	Always Occurs
9. Difficulty in presenting ideas clearly due to lack of organization		✓	
10. Fear of not being interesting		After ✓ performance	
11. Fear of being judged by the audience		✓	
12. Fear of making a solo performance	✓		
13. Fear of not having answers during the Q/A session			✓
14. Other:			

Check List #2

As Bob has done, you should take a serious look at your feelings and attitudes toward public speaking. What are some of the "blocks" that get in your way?

Put a check in the column that best describes how frequently your stumbling blocks occur. If a particular block never occurs, leave the column blank.

STUMBLING BLOCKS	Seldom Occurs	Frequently Occurs	Always Occurs
1. Fear of not knowing the audience's predisposition toward you or your message.			
2. Lack of self-confidence			
3. Feeling of over-confidence			
4. Nervousness			
5. Loss of control			
6. Inability to be conversational			
7. Fear of not having enough data to support your points			
8. Feeling that you have to use exact language, and fearing that you will not be able to find a word			

STUMBLING BLOCKS	Seldom Occurs	Frequently Occurs	Always Occurs
9. Difficulty in presenting ideas clearly due to lack of organization			
10. Fear of not being interesting			
11. Fear of being judged by the audience			
12. Fear of making a solo performance			
13. Fear of not having answers during the Q/A session			
14. Other:			

As the authority on communication, Wonder Word understands the negative impact that common fears and frustrations can have when you are presenting ideas in a formal format—especially when public speaking is not a routine event for you. But, whether giving a pre-planned speech or speaking spontaneously in an informal atmosphere, everyone has past experiences on which to build. Some people have a natural flair for humor; others have interesting vocal quality; yet others have a natural ability to organize their messages and choose precise, illustrative language. Each and every one of us has specific talents that can apply to public speaking situations. By examining past experiences, your strengths and weaknesses as a speaker are revealed.

Ⓦ   Bob, now that we've discussed your common stumbling blocks, what areas do you handle well in a presentational mode?

BE: Wonder Word, I hate to be repetitive, but there's nothing I do well during a presentation. I question whether I can, in fact, improve. I've been this way for too long.

Ⓦ   You *can* improve quite easily and that's my purpose here—to assist you in changing your public speaking style. To do that we first must examine your other speaking situations. There must be some that were positive.

BE: No—I've never liked it.

Ⓦ   How about your weekly marketing reports—or don't you consider that public speaking?

BE: Well, of course that's not public speaking! That's part of my job.

Ⓦ   Do you stand before the group? Do you ask listeners to hold questions until you complete your report? Do you organize your ideas before you present them clearly? Do you use visual aids to clarify your message?

BE: Sure I do, but meetings are my forte.

Ⓦ   Did you ever consider that the elements you use to effectively present your ideas in meetings are the same elements you use for more formal public speaking situations? The only difference is the size of your audience and how you feel about the two different forums. By analyzing all of your speaking experiences, you can discover areas of strength and isolate specific weaknesses. Once you have identified your individual needs, you can set realistic objectives to direct your development as a public speaker. Have you ever thought about what you want to accomplish when you speak?

BE: Of course. I want to be excellent, dynamic, effective . . .

Ⓦ A worthy list of adjectives. But to achieve this ultimate goal you must focus on the specific elements of speaking that will aid you in becoming all of the descriptive terms you recited. You need to complete the presentational skills survey.

Presentational Skills Survey

Name *Bob Emerson*

Part I

1. How frequently must you present your ideas at meetings that you attend?

   Always

2. Of the times you must present your ideas, how often must those ideas be presented in a formal fashion? (Formal is defined as a pre–planned presentation delivered in a standing posture.)

   Once a week in the marketing meeting.

3. Do you ever give presentations in environments other than meetings? (i.e. sales presentations, training sessions)

   Yes, conferences

4. Who are your audiences? (i.e. peers, subordinates, superiors, customers)

   Superiors, peers, customers

5. What is the size range of your various audiences?

   5–125

6. Do you use visual aids? If yes, list the types you use. If no, why?

   Yes, only in management meetings. I use overheads.

7. Have you had formal presentational training? If so, what type of program?

   Yes, evening program at the local university.

8. What do you find most difficult when making a formal presentation?

   Controlling nervousness.

9. What do you find least difficult when making a formal presentation?

   Dealing with informational questions.

10. Are you ever required to read your presentations? If yes, how often would this occur?

    Yes, once a year when delivering a slide show at the annual management meeting.

Part II

In column A, please rate on a scale of 0–5 (5 as the highest rating), the degree to which you exhibit the following skills and knowledge.

	A
Control nervousness when delivering a stand–up presentation	0
Read nonverbal audience feedback	2
Adapt to audience nonverbal feedback	2
Analyze audience prior to presentation	3
Organize your presentation	2
Initiate and maintain audience interest	1
Use appropriate language	4
Deal with hostile questions	3
Deal with informational questions	4
Use visual aids	4
Read a manuscript	2
Introduce a speaker	3

BE: Filling out the questionnaire helped me to see how frequently I do present my ideas. I can see for the first time that I do have some basic skills. Rating my skills helps me to view my strengths and weaknesses in a more realistic fashion. From my own survey I would say I need to focus on controlling my nervousness and improving my response to the audience. This means I need to create more interest, and learn to read the audience and adjust my message accordingly. Also, I like to listen to speakers who look relaxed, use gestures, and move about in a natural fashion. When I present, I either grip the podium or look like I'm directing the band. I want to achieve a style that looks professional, and is also comfortable for me.

Ⓦ You've listed several areas for development, Bob. To determine where we should concentrate our efforts, I've created an objective measurement chart. It will allow you to weigh the importance of each objective.

Objective Measurement Chart

Review the objectives listed below. Determine and weigh those that are important for you to achieve with the guidance of this book.

OBJECTIVES	√	DEGREE OF IMPORTANCE	DEGREE OF FULFILLMENT
Check those objectives that are important to you. Ignore those that are not.		Weight each objective checked for its importance to you. A total of 100 points must be assigned.*	Following completion of book, rate each checked objective from 1–10 to indicate degree of fulfillment.**
1. To control nervousness	√	60	
2. To establish audience rapport	√	10	
3. To adapt communication style	√	5	
4. To use gestures that complement the verbal message	√	5	
5. To maintain audience interest	√	15	
6. To present an organized speech		N/A	
7. To be adequately prepared		N/A	
8. To effectively handle question & answer sessions	√	5	

*If you checked only one objective, assign all 100 points. If you checked two objectives, spread the 100 points between them.

** 0	= unsatisfactory	5	= average	7	= good
1–2	= poor	6	= above average	8	= very good
3–4	= below average	N/A	= not applicable	9–10	= excellent

Bob has identified the areas he needs to work on, and has set his objectives accordingly. Each speaker has individual needs. For some, it may take only a minor change such as learning to control one element of the presentation, i.e., presenting a message in an organized fashion. For most, however, several changes need to occur.

Complete the Presentational Skills Survey to assist you in identifying your strengths and weaknesses as a presenter. Then, complete the objectives measurement chart.

Presentational Skills Survey

Name_____

Part I

1. How frequently must you present your ideas at meetings that you attend?

2. Of the times you must present your ideas, how often must those ideas be presented in a formal fashion? (Formal is defined as a pre–planned presentation delivered in a standing posture.)

3. Do you ever give presentations in environments other than meetings? (i.e. sales presentations, training sessions)

4. Who are your audiences? (i.e. peers, subordinates, superiors, customers)

5. What is the size range of your various audiences?

6. Do you use visual aids? If yes, list the types you use. If no, why?

7. Have you had formal presentational training? If so, what type of program?

8. What do you find most difficult when making a formal presentation?

9. What do you find least difficult when making a formal presentation?

10. Are you ever required to read your presentations? If yes, how often would this occur?

Part II

In column A, please rate on a scale of 0–5 (5 as the highest rating), the degree to which you exhibit the following skills and knowledge.

	A
Control nervousness when delivering a stand-up presentation	___
Read nonverbal audience feedback	___
Adapt to audience nonverbal feedback	___
Analyze audience prior to presentation	___
Organize your presentation	___
Initiate and maintain audience interest	___
Use appropriate language	___
Deal with hostile questions	___
Deal with informational questions	___
Use visual aids	___
Read a manuscript	___
Introduce a speaker	___

Objective Measurement Chart

Review the objectives listed below. Determine and weigh those that are important for you to achieve with the guidance of this book.

OBJECTIVES	√	DEGREE OF IMPORTANCE	DEGREE OF FULFILLMENT
Check those objectives that are important to you. Ignore those that are not.		Weight each objective checked for its importance to you. A total of 100 points must be assigned.*	Following completion of book, rate each checked objective from 1–10 to indicate degree of fulfillment.**
1. To control nervousness			
2. To establish audience rapport			
3. To adapt communication style			
4. To use gestures that complement the verbal message			
5. To maintain audience interest			
6. To present an organized speech			
7. To be adequately prepared			
8. To effectively handle question & answer sessions			

*If you checked only one objective, assign all 100 points. If you checked two objectives, spread the 100 points between them.

** 0 = unsatisfactory	5 = average	7 = good
1–2 = poor	6 = above average	8 = very good
3–4 = below average	N/A = not applicable	9–10 = excellent

Summary

In order to determine where to go, you first need to assess where you've been. This step was accomplished through a needs analysis. The analysis involved two procedures: first, identification of your stumbling blocks to public speaking and second, evaluation of your previous speaking situations. The analysis was also designed to assist you in setting your own personal objectives. By identifying these factors, you are better able to use the techniques and procedures that are discussed throughout this book.

Implementation of these techniques provides a means for overcoming or controlling common stumbling blocks. For example, as stated, many people experience fear of public speaking. This fear is sometimes manifested as nervousness. Through use of controlling techniques, nervousness is eliminated as a stumbling block. Oh yes, nervousness will continue to exist, but it will exist as positive energy rather than as negative energy.

One of the first means of gaining control is through understanding how the audience listens. Read on as Wonder Word develops an awareness in Bob of the communication process and the tools with which people communicate.

CHAPTER TWO

WHEN YOU SPEAK, CAN YOUR AUDIENCE LISTEN?

A speaker adjusting the microphone before launching into a presentation usually asks, "Can everyone *hear* me?" We all understand that in order to comprehend information, the first element involved is to hear the message, accurately and clearly.

Hearing is a *passive,* or reactive process. Listening, on the other hand, is very much an *active* one. In order to understand the many barriers that interfere with listening, it is important to examine *how* people listen. Since people listen with all their senses, it is necessary to control our verbal, nonverbal, and paralinguistic communication to reinforce the message and reduce both psychological and physical barriers. Wonder Word explained to Bob how we listen:

Ⓦ In the "good old days," Bob, most people were listeners. In other words, they would force themselves to focus primarily on the verbal message. Well-disciplined, intellect-style communicators may have the ability to concentrate in this manner, but I've found that, increasingly, a great percentage of audiences *watch* the speaker; that is, they are attentive to the nonverbal as well as verbal messages communicated by the speaker. As our society communicates more and more on a visual level, audiences are more attuned to this element of communication, and become watchers, rather than listeners.

Research has confirmed this phenomenon. A recent study published in the *Harvard Business Review,* (November–December, 1979), stated that up to 87 percent of our messages are interpreted on a nonverbal level. All messages are processed by our senses— our eyes, nose, touch and taste sensors, as well as by our ears. One reason that visual messages have such a strong impact is that the optical nerve endings are closer to the brain than the auditory nerve fibers. Thus, visual messages travel faster and are recognized sooner by the brain.

The various elements that create communication can generally be divided into three categories: verbal, nonverbal, and paralinguistic communication.

ELEMENTS OF COMMUNICATION

Verbal

- Language choice
    Type of language
    Tentative, non-specific language
    Technical terminology
    Colloquialisms
    Formal vs. informal
    Illustrative language
- Organization of message
    Main point first
    Main point last
    Overview of information
- Verbal interest elements
    Stories
    Jokes
    Analogies
    Quotations

Nonverbal

- Dress, attire
    Formal vs. informal
    Power vs. passive
- Gestures
    Body movement
    Hand gestures
    Postures
    Facial gestures
- Use of space
    Walking patterns
    Postures
    Power vs. passive
- Physical characteristics
    Height
    Weight
    Build
    Signs of aging
    Male/female

- Nonverbal interest elements
   Visual aids

Paralinguistic

- Tone
- Rate
- Pitch
- Intonation
- Accents
- Extra noises (laughter, cough, ums, ers, uhs)

Ⓦ   Not only are we sensitive to both verbal and nonverbal signals, but also we rely heavily on paralinguistic signals. If you say to me, "I really enjoy this conversation" in a monotonous and low tone, I would suspect your interests were elsewhere. However, if you said that in an animated voice, accenting the word *really,* and ending on an exclamatory note, I would feel confident that you appreciated the value of my words.

BE: I *really* am enjoying this conversation, Wonder Word!

Ⓦ   Practice is covered in a later chapter, Bob.

The point is, that even if we prefer to focus our attention on the verbal message alone, it is an impossible task. We process these other signals continuously, often subconsciously, so that we are unaware of why we react as we do. Have you ever listened to a speech and reacted negatively without knowing the reason? It is probably a result of nonverbal messages that you have processed and refuted on a subconscious level. Therefore, when we communicate, we need to consider and utilize all three areas.

BE: And all along I thought people just listened! I can't get over how complex communication really is.

Ⓦ   Speaking of communication, Bob—what does "communication" mean to you? In this world of telecommunications, communication systems, oral communication, written communication, communication gaps, etc., you might be tempted to avoid the whole process. Yet we communicate because we have information to deliver, an idea to share, or action to request. Bob, your intention

*In communication, feedback is essential for the sender to understand how the
receiver is receiving the message.*

was to persuade users of Watson machines to switch to the up-
graded computerized machinery. We are all called upon to communicate various messages in the performance of our professional and
social responsibilities. What actually takes place?

BE: I'm not so sure anymore, Wonder Word. Can you explain it?

Ⓦ   Of course! The communication process has four key elements:
- The *sender* is the source of the message.
- The *message* is the translation of ideas into words, gestures, paralinguistics, and visualization.
- The *receiver* is the individual for whom the information is targeted.
- The *feedback* is the translation of response into words, gestures, paralinguistics and visualization.

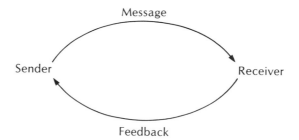

The Communication Process

Ideally, the communication process is a continuous flow or cycle of
message transmission. The receiver response, provided through feedback, affects the sender by indicating how the message is being received.
A speaker must continually register feedback and decide how to act
upon it. For example, a number of furrowed brows in the audience
could indicate 1) deep thought, 2) difficulty understanding, or 3) negative reaction to the message. In response, the speaker may need to de-
crease his or her rate of delivery, ask questions of the audience, define
terminology, pause to indicate main points, or restate the message for
clarity. Even in a public speaking situation where there is no verbal feedback, a speaker can and *must* be attuned to audience response. Feedback is one of the most powerful tools of control that a speaker has.

Communication must be adapted to fit the needs of the participants and their listening situation.

To illustrate the difficulty in delivering a message without benefit of feedback, try this simple exercise:

Listening Exercise

Wonder Word demonstrated this listening exercise with Bob: you can corner a friend or colleague. Ask him or her to spend a few moments with you to demonstrate the impact of feedback on both the message sender and receiver. Provide your partner with a blank paper and pen. Sit back-to-back. Now refer to the geometric illustration below. Your objective is to direct your partner in duplicating the design. Directions should be given for one line at a time; you may use angles, degrees, right/left, north, south, east, west orientation, and inches, but not geometric forms (triangles, squares, etc.). For example, you might say, "Go to the top of the page, 1 inch down from the top, 2 inches in from the left side—put your pen on the paper and draw a straight line down to within 4 inches of the bottom." The illustrator cannot ask any questions; you proceed as you consider it appropriate.

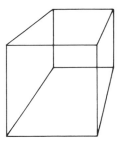

How did you do?

Were you frustrated as the sender?

How did you convey your frustration (tone of voice, language)?

Was the listener frustrated?

What impeded listening for him/her?

Wonder Word would recommend trying another approach.

Try another design. This time, the receiver can ask one question per direction.

Were the results more accurate?

Were you less frustrated as the sender?

Did you change directions, language, or tone as a result of feedback?

How did the listener react?

How did the listener overcome any barriers?

In numerous workshop experiences using this exercise, it has been found that without the opportunity to provide or interpret feedback, *both* participants experience varying degrees of frustration. Also, because there is no feedback, the sender is not aware of why or how to adapt his message. Thus, if a receiver has difficulty listening to sender language choice, or style of organization, or a certain paralinguistic manifestation, he cannot relay this response in any way to the sender.

No feedback = no adaption of message = potential frustration.

Returning to Bob and Wonder Word . . .

Ⓦ   Bob, it takes experience and guidance to know how to interpret and respond to audience feedback. Most speakers feel that when they communicate a message, the receiver will understand it and assimilate the information exactly as they intended it. Unfortunately, this is rarely the case. Barriers obstruct both the message and feedback, and impede the listening ability of your audience.

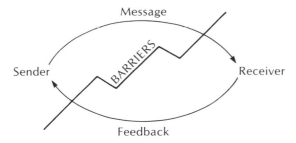

Barriers can prevent communication from being successful.

BE: Please speak up, Wonder Word, the cleaning crew is at it again!

Ⓦ   I had them come back to illustrate my point, Bob. I'm in charge here. Barriers to effective listening occur on a physical and psychological level. They affect the degree to which the receiver hears, understands, and retains the message. Physical barriers relate to you and how you feel, the speaker (how he or she looks, acts), and the environment. Psychological barriers (conscious or subconscious) exist as a result of background, predispositions, and established feelings and beliefs. People hear what they want to hear and expect to hear. If an idea or message reflects your personal knowledge and opinions, you are likely to accept and believe it. The greater the divergence from your accepted beliefs, the lesser the probability that you will react positively to the message.

BE: That's why I got such a poor response from customer service when I presented our new strategy for cross–selling other products to existing customers.

(W) Exactly, Bob. They didn't perceive themselves as sales people. That information did not fit into their system of beliefs. Several factors influence our listening ability. Examine the following information on the psychological and physical barriers that affect message assimilation.

The barriers that obstruct listening occur in four separate stages:

I. Response to speaker
   A. Distracting characteristics
      1. voice
      2. dress
      3. style of delivery
      4. lack of credibility
      5. over– or under–gesturer
   B. Predispositions about speaker
      1. personal
      2. company
      3. social/racial/economic

II. Response to message:
   A. Negative reaction
      1. boring, easy, rote, inappropriate
      2. too difficult, complicated
      3. emotional language
   B. Thought process
      1. thought rate faster than speech rate
         (mind wanders, becomes easily distracted)
      2. rebuttal, questioning, or elaborating on message internally

    C. Note–taking process
      1. overly thorough, miss major points
      2. listen only for facts, miss general meaning

III. Response to environment:
    A. Noise
    B. Interruptions
    C. Temperature
    D. Time of day

IV. Personal barriers:
    A. Fatigue
    B. Sickness
    C. Hunger
    D. Tension
    E. Negative attitude

BE: Wonder Word, I may never speak again. I never knew what I was up against!

Ⓦ Don't despair, Bob. In spite of all these barriers, if you are interesting and if your presentation is topical, you can surmount many barriers in order to effectively transmit your message. Last time, however, you didn't fare so well. After your presentation, I asked George Fullam, one of your oldest clients, if he would complete a simple audience reaction questionnaire. This is how he reacted to your talk, Bob.

BE: Do I have to look, Wonder Word?

AUDIENCE REACTION QUESTIONNAIRE

1.	Did you have any conscious predisposition toward the speaker?	<u>yes</u>	no
	the topic?	yes	<u>no</u>
2.	If yes, was your attitude negative?	yes	<u>no</u>
3.	Did you notice any distracting element in the speaker's delivery?	<u>yes</u>	no
4.	Did you miss or have difficulty following the main points of the talk?	<u>yes</u>	no
5.	Were you aware of any nervousness on the part of the speaker?	<u>yes</u>	no

6. Did you feel that the speaker was able to relate to
   the audience?   yes   <u>no</u>
7. Did you become bored as a listener?   yes   <u>no</u>
8. Did the speaker use any interest elements during
   the presentation?   yes   <u>no</u>
9. Can you remember the main issues discussed?   yes   <u>no</u>
10. Did you primarily *watch* rather than *listen*?   <u>yes</u>   no

George enjoyed Bob as a marketing representative and had a positive attitude about him when he began his presentation. And because of this favorable predisposition, George tried really hard to follow the topic; but since there were so many points, George became confused as to the real objective of Bob's talk, and was unable to recall the information. To his surprise, George discovered that, although he prided himself on his listening skills, he found himself *watching* Bob, rather than listening to him.

The next time you hear a presentation, discover what type of listener you are by completing this survey:

1. Did you have any conscious predisposition about
   the speaker?   yes   no
   the topic?   yes   no
2. If yes, was your attitude negative?   yes   no
3. Did you notice any distracting element in the
   speaker's delivery?   yes   no
4. Did you miss or have difficulty following the
   main points of the talk?   yes   no
5. Were you aware of any nervousness on the part of
   the speaker?   yes   no
6. Did you feel that the speaker was able to relate to
   the audience?   yes   no
7. Did you become bored as a listener?   yes   no
8. Did the speaker use any interest elements during
   the presentation?   yes   no
9. Can you remember the main issues discussed?   yes   no
10. Did you primarily *watch* rather than *listen*?   yes   no

Summary

As a speaker, you are concerned about creating a positive listening environment for your audience so that they can hear your message as accurately as possible. Messages are composed of three primary elements—verbal, nonverbal, and paralinguistic—which operate simultaneously and affect us on conscious and subconscious levels. One way that an audience can control communication is to provide feedback to the speaker so that he or she can adjust his message. Lack of feedback hinders a speaker's ability to effectively communicate his message.

Another impediment to the communication process is the existence of psychological and physical barriers produced by the speaker, the message, the environment, and the personal state of the receiver. In order to understand how others may respond to you as a presenter, it is important to identify your own listening habits.

CHAPTER THREE

WHAT ABOUT NERVOUSNESS?

As the most knowledgeable authority on communication, Wonder Word has been asked on numerous occasions to eliminate the nervousness that a person experiences when required to speak before a group. His response has always been, and still is, *never*! Wonder Word would never eliminate nervousness completely. Why? Because nervousness creates the necessary edge to make a presentation spontaneous and exciting. However, if nervousness becomes your *focus*, failure is guaranteed. You can't breathe, your hands shake uncontrollably and your voice cracks, so giving a dynamic presentation is impossible.

The key to handling nervousness is controlling the symptoms of panic while channeling your nervous energy creatively. This chapter helps you achieve that balance. First you identify the symptoms you manifest: then Wonder Word gives you the three methods for controlling those symptoms while keeping your creative spark.

The following is a symptom identification sheet that Bob filled out subsequent to his presentation at the technicians' conference.

SYMPTOM IDENTIFICATION

Answer each of the questions listed below.

1. Briefly describe a presentation situation that you have recently been involved in when you experienced anxiety. Describe problem areas.

Presented a new product line to audience of 100 technicians at a conference. Used a microphone and a podium, both for the first time. Had never met any of the audience members before.

2. Check the column to the right, indicating your anxiety symptoms, and list when they occur.

	Occurs before presentation	Occurs during presentation
Tight chest	X	
Rapid heart beat	X	
Excessive sweating	X	
Breathing difficulty	X	
Loss of thoughts	X	X
Downward-cast eyes		X
Excessive fluid in mouth	X	X
Too little fluid in mouth		
Verbal pause		X
Clearing throat	X	X
Change in vocal pitch		X
Increase in vocal rate		X
Audible shallow breathing	X	X
Physical twitches, list: *twirled hair*		X
Physically static–gripped podium		X

Now it's your turn. Fill out the symptom identification sheet on the next page. What presentations bring out your nervous symptoms and what are those symptoms? Once you know that, Wonder Word can give guidelines to help you control your nervous manifestations.

SYMPTOM IDENTIFICATION

Answer each of the questions listed below.

1. Briefly describe a presentation situation that you have recently
    been involved in when you experienced anxiety. Describe problem
    areas.

    _____

    _____

    _____

    _____

2. Check the column to the right, indicating your anxiety symptoms
    and list when they occur.

	Occurs before presentation	*Occurs during presentation*
Tight chest		
Rapid heart beat		
Excessive sweating		
Breathing difficulty		
Loss of thoughts		
Downward-cast eyes		
Excessive fluid in mouth		
Too little fluid in mouth		
Verbal pauses		
Clearing of throat		
Change in vocal pitch		
Increase in vocal rate		
Audible shallow breathing		
Physical twitches, list:		
Physically static–gripped podium		

There are three methods you can use to control your nervous symptoms: proper preparation, physical controls, and mental strategies. Let's take a look at how Bob could have avoided his panic–stricken experience by using the following techniques:

Ⓦ Bob, what steps could you have taken while preparing that would have lessened some of the nervousness you experienced?

BE: Nothing. I organized my thoughts. I practiced the night before. How was I supposed to know I'd get so nervous when I saw all of those people?

Ⓦ Did you know how many people were expected to attend the conference?

BE: Well, no.

Ⓦ How many *had* you anticipated?

BE: Oh, around forty or fifty.

Ⓦ Do you think it would have helped to know what you were dealing with?

BE: I never thought of that.

Ⓦ Obviously. Another thing—wasn't that the first time you used a microphone?

BE: Yes, and it really intimidated me. I thought I had to be professional *plus*. And I certainly didn't expect it to whine at me.

Ⓦ And didn't that add to your nervousness?

BE: Of course, but—I wasn't aware that I would need to use a mike.

Ⓦ *Preparation,* Bob, *Preparation.* All you had to do was make a phone call to find out the number of people attending, and the meeting set-up. Then you could have made a point of practicing your presentation using a podium and a microphone. Another bit of information you could have used was the time for which your presentation was slotted.

BE: Now you're stretching it. How is knowing *when* I speak going to help me be less nervous?

Ⓦ Think back, Bob. When did you begin to get nervous?

BE: Well, I was fine until I realized how many people were there.

Ⓦ   But when did the anxiety really start to build?

BE: Hmm . . . I guess I got anxious as I started listening to the other speakers. The longer I sat there, the more nervous I became.

Ⓦ   Exactly. If you had known you were toward the end of the agenda, you could have arrived later, saving yourself a lot of unneeded anxiety. Not everyone gets nervous while waiting to speak, but since *you* do, arrange your schedule to accommodate *your own needs.*

BE: I never would have thought of that.

Ⓦ   I know, Bob. That's why you're the pupil and I'm the teacher. Now, about your claim of leaving yourself plenty of time to practice—

BE: Now just a second. So far everything you've said makes sense, but I *did* practice. That's one thing my course taught me. My notes were well thought out, my rehearsal in front of the mirror was great. I can't help it if a few nerves made me lose my train of thought.

Ⓦ   A simple miscalculation, Bob. One practice is never enough. By running through your presentation three or four times the likelihood of forgetting is reduced greatly. One run through does not allow you to absorb your thoughts and language patterns completely. Only repetition will do that. Also, you should have found someone to act as an audience. Even when presenting to one person, a little nervousness will show. Thus, you can begin to practice methods of masking nervous manifestations through physical controls.

BE: You know, Wonder Word, the one thing that really did get to me was how I *physically* reacted to being nervous. I almost felt like my body belonged to someone else.

Ⓦ   Once again, Bob, your reaction was typical. Although nervousness is caused by a mental lack of confidence, the body responds as if it were being threatened physically. In both situations the body is reacting to stress. Thus, the solution is to find physical means to control your body's physical reaction. The first thing that happens when reacting to stress is that your body pumps out excessive adrenalin. Now, if you were being threatened physically, that excess adrenalin would provide the energy and strength needed to run or fight back. However, when you are presenting your ideas, that excess adrenalin begins to create problems.

BE: You're telling me!

(W) Let me tell you more! The excess adrenalin increases your heart rate, thus increasing your breathing rate and the amount you perspire. As if that isn't enough, your muscles tighten up to prepare you for increased physical activity.

BE: I remember what happened to me, Wonder Word—the question is, how do I control myself?

(W) The first step is to process some of the excess adrenalin. One method is to move about before your presentation. Stand, stretch, or exercise. Not only will this work at the root of the problem —excess adrenalin—but it will also assist you in relaxing your muscles. The following simple exercises have worked for others. Why don't you give them a try?

1. Raise one hand up toward the ceiling and lower one hand toward the floor. Pretend to push up the ceiling and to push down the floor.
2. Now reverse arm positions.
3. Next, stretch arms out to the side and pretend to push the walls away from you.

4. Rotate head in a full circle keeping the remainder of your body stationary.
5. Reverse rotation direction.

6. With arms straight down and close to your sides, pull shoulders up as high as you can. Tense up, then relax.

BE: Well, Wonder Word, those really do help me to relax, but what if I don't have time to do these before a presentation?

Ⓦ Don't forget, you can move about during your presentation as well. Not only will this help you work off some of the adrenalin, but it will add interest to your presentation. But Bob, you need to be careful to direct the movement so you don't distract from the verbal presentation.

BE: You mean twirling my hair doesn't count?

Ⓦ That's right. A nervous twitch will distract the audience. If you know you have a tendency to pick your nails, twirl your hair, play with a ring or any of the thousands of other nervous quirks that can surface, be sure to adopt a posture to either hide that twitch or prevent it from happening. For example, since you only twirled your hair with your right hand, placing that hand in a pocket would eliminate the behavior.
Another technique you can use to relax is diaphragmatic breathing.

BE: Diafram-what?

Ⓦ Diaphragmatic breathing, Bob, is a technique that forces you to relax your diaphragm so oxygen can flow more freely to the lungs. In addition to helping you relax, this technique controls those nervous manifestations that are directly caused by lack of oxygen— you know, the tight feelings in your chest, the shallow breathing, the change in vocal pitch, even your lapses of memory.

BE: How can I ever forget those symptoms? I hope this works. How do I start?

1. Place your right hand on your stomach just above
2. Place your left hand on your chest.
3. Take a deep breath, pushing your stomach out. Your chest and shoulders should remain stationary.
4. Exhale, blowing out through your mouth. Repeat 3–4 times.

BE: One question, Wonder Word.

Ⓦ   Yes, Bob.

BE: You said that this method will help me with my lapses in memory. I can see how this will help me with the other nervous symptoms you mentioned, but how does this help me to *remember?*

Ⓦ   What you must understand is *why* you have lapses in memory. Although in your case it might be a natural phenomenon, for most people the reason is directly related to a lack of oxygen. By increasing the oxygen flow, the problem is minimized.

BE: Well, you seem to have covered physical controls from A to Z. You're really thorough, Wonder Word.

Ⓦ   Actually, there's one more.

BE: What's that?

Ⓦ   As you spoke, there were quite a few times when you had to pause to swallow or to clear your throat.

BE: That's true. I just couldn't seem to control the moisture in my mouth. But how could you possibly control that?

Ⓦ   It just so happens that you can. *Binaca,* a breath freshener, or citrus fruits, such as limes or lemons, act to keep the right amount of fluid in your mouth. Just before you stand up to present your ideas, put several drops of *Binaca* on the tip of your tongue, or order a cup of tea with lemon and suck on the lemon. These items will be effective for approximately 20 minutes.
Now that you understand physical controls, let's talk about mental strategies that will help combat nervousness. If you had been asked at a meeting to present the same thoughts that you presented at the conference, would you have been as nervous?

BE: Of course not. But that's a completely different situation.

Ⓦ   Is it really? In both situations you are presenting your ideas. In both situations you are receiving feedback from the participants in the interaction.

BE: In a meeting situation, I know the people and how to read their feedback. I'm comfortable with them. I felt exposed standing up in front of all of those strangers. I could just tell they were judging every move I made.

Ⓦ They were judging you no differently than how you are being judged every day. The difference is in how *you* view the interaction. By creating a sense of rapport with your audience, you can reduce your own anxiety. The strangers will become individuals, and the confidence you display in meetings will be transferred to the more formal environment.

BE: That sounds good, but how can you establish rapport with a group of total strangers in a half-hour presentation?

Ⓦ There are several techniques you can use. Did you ever focus on anyone in the audience?

BE: No, they all just seemed to melt together.

Ⓦ And when they fused together they were no longer individuals whom you were speaking *with*, but a mob that you were talking *at*. If you had established eye contact with one friendly face in the audience, then moved on to look at another friendly face, eventually you would have seen that mob become individuals. Your speech would have become just another conversation with your feedback being exclusively nonverbal.
Another technique you can use is to meet several participants prior to the presentation. That way you can address familiar faces. If you discover examples that illustrate your information, then refer to those incidents, and the individuals involved. Not only will this make you feel more attuned to your audience, but your audience will accept your message more readily.

BE: With the information you've given me, I don't think I'll ever be nervous again.

Ⓦ I wouldn't go *that* far. You'll never eliminate your initial nervousness completely. My intent is for you to control your nervous symptoms so that you are more comfortable and therefore in control.

Summary

Once you have identified the nervous symptoms you can select the techniques to control those symptoms.

I.   Prepare; the unexpected will be less likely to rattle you
   A.   Discover your presenting environment:
      1.   number of people attending
      2.   room set-up
      3.   time you are speaking
   B.   Allow time to practice

II .   Combat physical reactions to nervousness through physical controls
   A.   Move about before presentation
   B.   Move about during presentation
   C.   Hide nervous twitches
   D.   Use diaphragmatic breathing to increase oxygen flow, thus controlling the following nervous manifestations:
      1.   tight chest
      2.   shallow breathing
      3.   change in vocal pitch
      4.   lapses in memory
   E.   Use Binaca or citrus fruit to keep the right amount of moisture in your mouth

III.   Develop mental strategies
   A.   View as interpersonal conversation
   B.   Establish eye contact with friendly faces
   C.   Move eye contact as comfort level increases
   D.   Interact with audience prior to presentation
   E.   Make personal references to individuals within the audience

Remember—even the most seasoned, professional presenter gets nervous. But the professional *uses* the nervous energy to create spontaneity and spark. Now you can be like the pro. Use the positive aspects of nervousness without being overwhelmed by the negative.

CHAPTER FOUR

COMMUNICATING STYLES—YOU AND YOUR AUDIENCE

Many people have an image of what a good public speaker should be. Perhaps you're familiar with the stereotype: posture erect, one hand placed at the side; the other punching the air to stress an important point; head tilted back (to improve resonance when speaking). The introduction is a joke, the body of the speech covers three main points, and the conclusion inspires the audience to make a change. Works every time, right?

Well, only if: You know how to tell a joke.

Your topics always have three main points.

You have a flair for inspiring audiences to make a change.

AND

Your audience is always the same.

In other words, sometimes the formula works and sometimes it doesn't. Your success is balanced on three factors: your natural communication style, the predominant communication style of your audience, and your message.

People hear messages more easily from those who are similar to themselves. Thus, if you can learn to adapt elements of your style to match the style of your audience, your chances for being heard are increased. In addition, the intent of your message will be conveyed more effectively if your style is complementary.

In this chapter you will learn the various elements that create the four communication styles. You will discover how the elements differ from style to style and how some elements are the same. The goal will be for you to identify your primary style and the elements you exhibit from other styles. Future chapters will provide methods for identifying and adapting to various audience styles.

Let's listen in as Wonder Word helps Bob identify his primary style, while explaining to him the elements of the other three styles.

BE: You know, Wonder Word, I don't see what difference style makes. Seems to me that if I just learn how to present my ideas better, I'll be okay.

Ⓦ Well, Bob, that all depends on your definition of *better*.

BE: I would say better means more interesting, less nervous . . . just better than I did before.

Ⓦ That is one way to look at better, Bob. But I was looking at better from the audience's point of view. One audience might like humor, another might prefer a more statistical analysis, while another would prefer case studies that relate to their particular field. In each case the style of the audience would determine how best to present your ideas. That is why understanding your style is important. Unless you know your own style, how can you begin to adapt to meet the style of your audience?

BE: Good question, Wonder Word.

Ⓦ I rarely ask a bad one. Now, can we continue?

BE: Just one more thing. I don't see how I can adapt my style to the style of my audience. I'm not an actor.

Ⓦ Bob, perhaps if you thought about how you adapt your communication style naturally, then thinking about adapting for a presentation might be easier.

BE: But I can't adapt. I'm just me, Bob Emerson. I come across to everyone the same.

Ⓦ Think a little harder, Bob. Do you talk to your boss the same way you talk to your subordinates? Or do you talk to your car mechanic the same way you talk to the person who cuts your hair?

BE: Well, of course not.

Ⓦ Then whether you've ever realized it or not, you've been adapting your style to others for years. What you will learn is how to *consciously* adapt your communication style. But in order to learn how to adapt, you first need to know what the four styles are, and, more importantly, how you fit in.

BE: I thought you were interested in the individual. I object to putting people in categories.

Ⓦ The purpose of this exercise is to provide guidelines that describe your communicating behaviors. As I said before, you naturally adapt and change your behaviors according to the situation. My purpose is to put labels on those changes so that you are more able to consciously control those changes. I've compiled a list that gives a general description of the four styles of communication. As you read through it, notice whether any of them sound familiar.

Read through the descriptions with Bob. See if any of the characteristics listed fit *you*.

COMMUNICATION STYLES

Styles		General Descriptions
Passive:	Paralinguistic, verbal communication	Soft spoken with a slow rate; pauses frequently; uses tentative and general language; makes statements that sound like questions; organizes in recency fashion.
	Nonverbal communication	Uses passive postures, gestures rarely; when used, gestures are aimless; has large space limitation; clothes style is neutral to low authority.
	Motivation	Desires acceptance.
Amiable:	Paralinguistic, verbal communication	Medium speaking voice, with a medium rate; uses tentative language; uses general terms; uses descriptive terms; uses colloquial expressions; uses many personal examples; organizes in recency fashion.
	Nonverbal communication	Uses neutral postures; gestures frequently in an aimless fashion; has small space limitation; clothes style is neutral.
	Motivation	Desires affiliation.

Styles		**General Descriptions**
Intellect:	Paralinguistic, verbal communication	Soft to medium speaking voice, with a slow to medium rate; uses tentative language only when referring to data that is incomplete; uses multi-syllabic words; uses specific, technical terms; organizes in primacy fashion supporting every point with evidence.
	Nonverbal communication	Uses neutral postures; gestures rarely in a rigid fashion; has large space limitation; clothes style is neutral to high authority.
	Motivation	Desires achievement.
Driver:	Paralinguistic, verbal communication	Medium to loud speaking voice, with a fast rate; uses specific terms, uses descriptive terms; uses multi-syllabic words; organizes in recency fashion but prefers to hear information in a primacy fashion.
	Nonverbal communication	Uses authority postures; gestures frequently using illustrative gestures; has small space limitation; clothes style is high authority.
	Motivation	Desires control.

BE: I can tell by reading through all of the descriptions that you spent a great deal of time working out these different styles, Wonder Word. My only problem is that there are quite a few terms that I don't understand. So it's hard for me to decide which behaviors apply to me.

Ⓦ Don't worry, Bob. I knew we would have to review all of the elements that make up each of the styles, but I wanted you to at least get a general overview. Our next step will be to examine each element within the different styles.

BE: My first question is, what is *paralinguistics*?

ⓦ   *Paralinguistics* is the vocal part of communication, or in simpler terms, *how you say something.*

BE: You mean the emphasis I place on the words I use?

ⓦ   That's part of it, Bob. There are several categories in the area of paralinguistics. *Voice quality, volume, rate, pitch,* and *vocal pattern* are just a few. But we only look at two when examining the different styles. They are volume and rate. *Volume* is how loudly or softly a person speaks. *Rate* refers to the speed at which a person speaks. If you look back at the general styles description, you will notice that a *Passive* is characterized by a soft volume and a slow rate, the *Amiable* by a medium volume and a medium rate, the *Intellect* by a soft to medium volume and a slow to medium rate, the *Driver* by a medium to loud volume and a fast rate. In general, Bob, what do you think your volume and rate are?

BE: Hmm. I've been told I tend to get a little loud when I get excited. So I guess my volume is medium to loud. The rate part is easy—it's fast. I always feel like I have more to say than I have time to say it in. So far that makes me a Driver. Right?

ⓦ   YOU'VE GOT IT, Bob. To make a complete composite, I've created a grid for you to fill out. As we review each of the elements, make a note in the appropriate place on the grid. When we're finished you will have a complete breakdown of your communication style.

BE: What a unique idea. You certainly know how to make things easy.

ⓦ   I've had a lot of practice, Bob. *Years* of practice.

Have you been following Wonder Word's analysis? What do you think your volume and rate generally are? If you're not sure, ask a friend or a business associate. In fact, even if you are sure, ask a friend or business associate for a second opinion. Many times we think we communicate in a certain manner, but when we ask for feedback from others, we find they have a completely different perception from our own. The next page is a blank grid that you can fill out along with Bob, and Bob's completed grid can be found at the end of the chapter.

Communication Styles Grid

Communication Style	Paralinguistic Communication		Verbal Communication		Nonverbal Communication				
	Volume	Rate	Language Selection	Organization	Postures	Gestures	Space Limitations	Clothes Style	Motivation
Amiable									
Passive									
Intellect									
Driver									

Verbal communication is made up of two elements: the language you use and the way in which you organize your language. For you to determine your style, you need to understand the different types of language, the two methods of organizing, and, finally, how the different styles use both elements. The categories of language we will concern ourselves with are:

Tentative language	*Tentative* language is non–committal: "try," "perhaps," "maybe," "might," "may," and "sort of," are all examples of tentative language.
General language	*General* language is language that allows the listener a broad interpretation of meaning. Examples of general language are "the end of the day," "the middle of the month," and "as soon as possible."
Specific language	*Specific* language is the opposite of general language. Specific language limits the interpretation of meaning. Instead of "the end of the day," one would say "5:00 p.m." "The middle of the month" would be "the 15th" instead. "As soon as possible" would be exchanged for a realistic projection.
Descriptive language	*Descriptive* language is language that creates a picture for the listener. Examples are "rapid increase," "guttural laugh," and "bird's eye view."
Colloquial language	*Colloquial* language is language familiar to a particular region or group. An example of a *regional colloquialism* would be the word for carbonated soft drinks. In the Northeast the word is "tonic," on the West Coast the word is "soda," and in the Midwest the word is "pop." A *group colloquialism* can be characterized by different slang adopted by younger generations throughout the years. During the fifties something good was "keen," during the sixties it was "groovy," and during the seventies it was "far out."
Multi-syllabic words	*Multi-syllabic* words are exactly what they sound like—words with more than one syllable.
Technical language	*Technical* language is language used in a particular company or industry. For example, "90-day-notice account" is a term that is used in the banking industry.

Personal
language

Personal language consists of terms and examples used to involve the audience. Personal terms include individuals' names and personal pronouns. Personal examples are stories that involve the speaker or individual audience members.

Now that you know what the language categories are, and what they mean, let's go back to the general styles description and see how everything fits in. As we review the information, think about the type of language you use.

Turn back to the Communication Styles General Description. Review the language used by the four communication styles. Considering the language you normally use, which style fits you best? Once you've made your decision, write down the types of language you use in the proper style category on your Communication Style Grid. Refer to Bob's grid at the end of the chapter for a sample.

Ⓦ   What did you find out from the style grid, Bob?

BE: I discovered that Passives use tentative and general language. Amiables use tentative, general, descriptive, and colloquial language. Intellects use tentative language when they refer to data that is incomplete, multi-syllabic, specific, and technical language. Drivers use specific, descriptive, and multi-syllabic language.

Ⓦ   Very good, an excellent report. Now the more important question is, what type of language do *you* use and which style does that fit into?

BE: That's where I'm having trouble, Wonder Word. I use all different types of language. I can't determine exactly where I belong.

Ⓦ   Perhaps if I give you a sample, you'll be more able to make a decision. I'll select one phrase and show you how each of the different styles would say the phrase.

Sample phrase: Profits are increasing.

Passive: Profits have sort of increased, I think.
Amiable: Profits have really gone through the ceiling this past month.
Intellect: Profits have increased by 25 percent, meeting and exceeding our December projections.
Driver: Profits have leapt by 25 percent during the month of February alone.

BE: The difference is so striking when you put it that way.

Ⓦ   Exactly, Bob, so what do you think your language patterns are?

BE: I tend to use descriptive language. My wife always complains that she can never pin me down to a day or time to do chores around the house, so I guess I must use general language as well.

Ⓦ   So far, so good. What about personal references?

BE: I didn't think we were going to get personal, Wonder Word.

Ⓦ   And what do you call *we, you, us?*

BE: Oh. I guess you've got a point. Personal language must be a large part of my language pattern. The more I think about it, I also seem to use tentative language.

Ⓦ   When you put those all together, what style do you come up with for language?

BE: Amiable?

Ⓦ   Now you're talking! And we can proceed to *speech organization.* To help you visualize the difference between the two types of speech organization, please refer to Illustration IV A. The two methods of organization are called *recency* and *primacy. Recency* communicators give examples, statistics and other information that leads up to their main point. *Primacy* communicators give the main point, then give examples, statistics, and other information to support the main point.

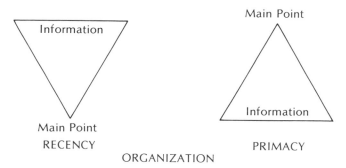

IVA. *Recency vs. Primacy Communication Organization*

BE: I've been cheating, Wonder Word. I've already looked back at my General Styles Description and I see that Amiables, Passives, and Drivers are all recency communicators. Seems like Intellects are the only ones that can get to the point right up front.

Ⓦ That's true, but don't overlook the one quirk Drivers have.

BE: Don't worry, I noticed that right away because that's my style. I always like to make sure I get out all my stories and facts before I get to my main idea, but if I have to listen to someone else do that, I *stop listening.*

Ⓦ That's right, Bob. Drivers are recency communicators, but they like to hear their messages in a primacy mode. Didn't I tell you organization would be simple?

BE: I'm starting to get used to your being right all the time.

Time to pull out your grid again. Are you predominantly a recency or a primacy communicator? Do you have a preference in how others communicate to you? Record your responses in the appropriate style category.

Ⓦ Nonverbal communication, like verbal communication, is comprised of several elements. We will analyze these areas as we did the verbal elements. First, we will discuss the different types of postures, gestures, space limitations and clothes styles, then subsequent to each discussion we will analyze how each element impacts style.

BE: That's what I like about you—primacy communicator through and through.

Ⓦ We're on nonverbal now, Bob. The first nonverbal signal to consider is the body posture. The body posture is categorized in three ways: high authority, neutral, and low authority. A description of each category is on the grid on the next page.

BE: After looking at the grid, I would say I tend to use authority postures a majority of the time.

Ⓦ Correct. So where does that place you in relationship to style?

BE: As I recall, Drivers use authority postures.

Body Posture Categories

Seated Posture	High Authority	Neutral	Low Authority
Torso position	Leaning back in chair, shoulders erect, occasionally leaning forward	Leaning back in chair, shoulders erect	Leaning back in chair, shoulders rounded or Leaning forward in chair, shoulders rounded
Hands	Resting on chair arms, or One arm resting on back of chair—or—hands clasped behind head	Hands resting on desk, or One hand resting on hip other hand resting on lap	Both hands folded resting on lap, or Both hands folded on desk
Legs and Feet	Legs crossed knee to knee Feet on desk	Legs crossed ankle to knee	Both feet on floor, resting together
Standing Posture			
Torso position	Shoulders erect	Shoulders erect	Shoulders rounded
Hands	Both hands on hips	Both hands in skirt or slacks pocket; One hand on hip, one hand resting at side; One hand resting behind back, one hand resting at side.	Both hands in front of body clasping each other; Both hands behind body clasping each other; Hands crossing body, resting at elbows.
Legs and Feet	Feet slightly apart, toes even, weight evenly distributed	One foot slightly in front of other, weight resting on back foot	Feet apart, toes uneven, weight shifting back and forth

58

(W)   Right. Let's see if you can evaluate your gestures as quickly. Gestures can be illustrative or aimless. Illustrative gestures mimic the language being used. If you were to say rising cost, your hand would move from a low point to a high point, illustrating the change. Aimless gestures have no purpose in relation to the language.

BE: I know I move my hands a lot when I talk, but they never seem to illustrate anything. The movement was just a way for me to get rid of some of my nervous energy. That puts me in the Amiable slot, according to the Styles Description.

(W)   As long as you're checking your description, how are the other styles portrayed?

BE: Passives rarely gesture, and when they do, the gestures are aimless. Intellects don't gesture much either, but the few that are used are illustrative. Drivers use frequent, illustrative gestures. So far, everything is understandable. But the next element of nonverbal communication really has me confused. What is a space limitation, and how does that affect communication?

(W)   A space limitation is an imaginary, portable territory each of us has along all the time. If other people move inside our space, we feel threatened. Our ability to listen and deliver accurate messages is lessened. One way to define your personal space is to observe the bend of your own elbow when you shake hands with a stranger for the first time. If you have a large space, your elbow will be fully extended. The more your elbow is bent, the smaller your space limitation. You can also judge personal space by observing your office or home environment. Those with large space limitations will have spartan furnishings with plenty of room to move about. Those with smaller space limitations tend to be more cluttered.

BE: That's fascinating. I'll have to remember to check my elbow the next time I shake hands with a stranger. Just looking at my personal surroundings, I would say I had a relatively small space limitation. According to the general description, that could fit in either a driver or an amiable style. Passives and intellects are just the opposite. They have large space limitations.

(W)   For not knowing anything about space limitation, you've caught on very quickly. Before you lose your momentum, we'll review the last element of nonverbal communication, *clothes style.* Clothes style is also split into three categories, but these categories are high authority, neutral, and low authority. The next two pages are grids listing the factors that create the different clothes style categories. Review the one for men, Bob, and tell me what you think.

BE: I'm definitely a high authority clothes style. My wife complains that the only color suits I own are navy blue and grey. I have to admit she's not too far from being right. Looks like I'm in the Driver category again.

(W)   Don't forget the other styles, Bob. Remember, you can use this information to help you identify your various audiences.

BE: Oh yes, the other styles. Passives have a neutral to low authority clothes style, amiables adopt a neutral style, and intellects have a neutral to high authority clothes style.

(W)   I couldn't have said it better myself.

Are you doing as well as Bob? Have you been able to identify the types of postures, gestures, space limitations and clothes style you use? Under what styles do the various elements fall? Are you beginning to see a primary style unfold? Before you make any final decisions, read about the last element that impacts your communication style.

(W)   Well, Bob, you have one space left to fill in on your communication styles grid.

BE: I know, Wonder Word. I read the general description and I know that the Passive desires acceptance, the Amiable desires affiliation, the Intellect desires achievement, and the Driver desires control and power over his environment.

(W)   Since you know all that, then you must know the answer to my next question. What is *your* motivation?

BE: I was afraid you were going to ask that. My problem is that I have mixed feelings. I feel a need to maintain control, yet I also need affiliation and friendships.

Men's Clothespower Grid

	High Authority	Neutral	Low Authority
Style	three-piece suit two-piece suit long sleeve shirt w/tie	slacks w/coordinating blazer long sleeve shirt w/tie	slacks w/shirt short sleeve shirt w/no tie
Material	wool wool blends linen linen blends	cotton cotton blends textured polyester	corduroy polyester

Color	navy blue
	charcoal-grey
	shirts—white
	    pale yellow
	    pale blue
		medium blue
		medium grey
		brown
		tan
			green
			pink
			bright yellow

Patterns	solids light pin stripe	small plaids	wide stripes large plaids
Tie	rep pattern insignia	solid small plaid	paisley
Shoes (always leather)	wing tips lace-ups	loafers slip on's w/tassel	boots
Jewelry	gold silver diamonds w/simple style	costume gold look silver look w/simple style	costume

Women's Clothespower Grid

	High Authority	Neutral	Low Authority
Style	two-piece skirted suit three-piece skirted suit blouse with closed neck and ascot	skirt w/coordinating blazer dress w/coordinating blazer open blouse	skirt w/blouse slacks w/blouse sweaters
Material	wool wool blends linen linen blends silk silk blends	cotton cotton blends textured polyester	corduroy polyester
Color	navy blue charcoal-grey blouses—white pale yellow pale blue	medium blue medium grey brown tan	red pink green lavender bright yellow
Patterns	solids light pin-striped	small plaids	flowers large plaids
Shoes (always leather)	closed toe medium heel	open toe sling pump	boots sandals high heels
Jewelry	gold silver diamonds w/simple style	costume gold look silver look w/simple style	costume

Ⓦ That doesn't seem so strange. If you look at your communication styles grid you'll see that your primary style is Driver but your secondary style is Amiable. Your motivations are still in line with the other elements of your communication style.

BE: What do you know? I'm right after all.

Ⓦ I must admit, Bob, you've outdone yourself when it comes to identifying the elements that create the four communication styles. And your assessment of your own style is accurate as well. I hope in future chapters you prove as capable at adapting to your various audiences.

Bob has completed his communication style grid. Have you completed yours? After you've filled in the last column, you can evaluate your primary and secondary communication style. Count the number of elements in each style column. The column with the greatest number is your primary style. The column with the second largest number is your secondary style.

Communication Styles Grid

Communication Style	Paralinguistic Communication		Verbal Communication		Nonverbal Communication				Motivation
	Volume	Rate	Language Selection	Organization	Postures	Gestures	Space Limitations	Clothes Style	
Amiable			descriptive, general, colloquial, and tentative			gestures frequently in an aimless fashion	small		desires affiliation
Passive									
Intellect				delivers in recency, prefers to listen to primacy	authority				
Driver	medium to loud	fast					small	high authority	desires control

Summary

Bob has just taken the first step in learning to adapt to various audiences. His task was to identify his style of communication. Along with Bob, you should now have an understanding of the various elements that determine communication style. Based on these elements, identification of your natural style should be complete.

The involved process of style identification included:

- Paralinguistic expressions
    vocal volume
    rate of speech
- Verbal communication
    language selection
    message organization
- Nonverbal communication
    postures
    gestures
    space
    clothing
- Motivation
    affiliation
    acceptance
    achievement
    power

For easy reference, four category headings were used to assist with the identification process: Passive, Amiable, Intellect and Driver. Salient features of the Passive style, for example, include a slow rate, soft volume, tentative language, general language, recency organization format, few gestures, and neutral clothing. Passives also desire acceptance. Each of the four above styles was discussed in depth.

Bob eventually came to the conclusion that his primary style of communication was Driver. Upon review of each element, he discovered that he spoke rapidly and loudly, and delivered information in the recency mode. Bob assumed authoritative postures, wore high authority clothing and was motivated by control.

Through analysis, Bob also determined that his secondary style of communication was Amiable since the areas not categorized as Driver represented the Amiable style.

Proceed with Bob as he discovers how his natural style affects others, and discover the techniques for adapting to various audiences.

CHAPTER FIVE

WHO'S OUT THERE?

Who is your audience? What do you need to know in order to be effective? Imagine arriving at a speaking engagement dressed in a navy pin-striped suit, with visual aids large enough to be viewed by twenty–five people. Your prepared speech contains a humorous joke about the Nixon administration and is interspersed with a lot of technical jargon. You are introduced, and stand before a Republican audience of seventy-five. They are dressed in casual attire and unfamiliar with your technical terms. Your chances of being effective are 0 to none! Conducting an audience analysis is clearly a definite prerequisite for any successful presentation. By knowing your audience, you can turn disinterested and seemingly growling faces into open and attentive ones. But you may ask, as Bob did—how?

When conducting an audience analysis, examine the 5 W's:

1. *Why have you been asked to speak?*
   Determine your objectives and select the appropriate type of speech.
2. *Who will be in your audience?*
   The composition of your audience will determine the manner in which your speech is delivered. (i.e. an Intellect audience receives information best from another Intellect.)
3. *When will you speak?*
   If you're fourth in an agenda of speakers, then be prepared for an audience that is fading out from overload.
4. *Where will you speak, and how many people will you address?*
   Your selection of visual aids is contingent upon this information, as are the support items you need to enhance your message.
5. *What will you be speaking on, and what will your viewpoint be?*

BE: All right, Wonder Word. You've shown me techniques on how to control my own nervousness and I know I'm a Driver/Amiable style. But this knowledge would have done absolutely nothing to help me through my opening. You remember, the microphone began to whine, my joke died, people began to whisper in the back, and the final insult was when a few people actually stood up and left right in the middle of my presentation.

Ⓦ   How could I forget?

BE: The question is, what will prevent those things from happening to me in the future?

(W) Just some common sense steps, Bob. Do you recall discussing the fact that you didn't get there before your session began in order to check the equipment—or that you didn't think through and test your joke out on the right people before you used it? Or, since you were the last speaker, you should have prepared yourself and integrated additional interest elements into your organization to keep their attention?

BE: It's very difficult to forget when you keep reminding me. My problem is, I don't understand what you're getting at.

(W) The point is—that you need to determine the factors that will affect the audience you will be talking to and tailor the development of your presentation based on that analysis—which leads me to what audience analysis is all about. Let's first consider *why* you had been asked to speak. Do you know why?

BE: I was selected, according to my boss, because I did much of the marketing research for the product. I know more about it than anyone else, except for the actual developers of the product. That's why Mr. Watson asked me to represent the company at the conference.

(W) No Bob, I fully understand why Mr. Watson selected you—but rather *why are you speaking? Why did the users want someone from Watson, Inc.?* And secondly, how would you benefit from speaking there?

BE: We were invited to inform the users about the new products available to them from Watson, Inc.

(W) That was your overt reason for speaking. But what should your underlying objective have been?

BE: To make the users aware of the product so they will buy it.

(W) *Exactly.* You were, on the surface, informing them, but your real reason for being there was to sell them on computerized machinery from Watson, Inc.

BE: So, I assume that you're telling me that the next time I speak I should first consider why I've been asked. Then, I should consider what my personal objective is and integrate the two. Right?

Ⓦ   Excellent! Excellent! Now, let's consider the who, when, where, and what of it all.

The next series of steps includes finding out 1) *Who* you will be speaking to, 2) *When* you will actually be speaking, 3) *Where* you will be speaking, and 4) *What* you will be talking about.

BE: Wait . . . wait a minute, Wonder Word, it sounds like a "W's" Convention. Sounds like I'll be spending endless hours researching the 5 W's. I think I should primarily worry about planning exactly what I'll be saying. Besides, I can't waste all that time; I don't get paid for making speeches!

Ⓦ   Oh, *really*? Consider your last presentation—who was your audience?

BE: Customers.

Ⓦ   And who buys your products so you can get paid?

BE: Customers.

Ⓦ   Precisely. Every time you speak you are representing yourself, as well as your company. The image you leave with your audience is important. Can you see that, Bob?

BE: I think so. But I don't have that much time to check all those things out.

Ⓦ   All it takes is one or two phone calls and perhaps a quick trip to the location where you'll be speaking.

BE: What phone calls? What would I say?

Ⓦ   Once you find out the who, you need to identify what style of audience you will be speaking to. Remember, in the last chapter we identified that each of us has a primary communication style. Not only do individuals exhibit specific behaviors, but remember that audiences also take on communication styles *as groups.* For example, sales types and executives—as a *group*, mind you—tend to take on a Driver tone. Your technical, manufacturing, engineer types, financial people, and lawyers all tend to fall into an intellect tone as an audience. Personnel people, middle management types, tend to become Amiables as an audience. And finally, support staff frequently take on a passive tone.

BE: Wonder Word, audiences are *so* diverse—every group must represent *all* communication styles. How can you generalize like that?

Ⓦ Lots of experience, Bob—*lots*. Let's examine your audience to prove my point. Describe the various people represented in your audience.

BE: Well . . they are all customers of ours.

Ⓦ I realize that, but rather, what departments are they part of in their representative companies?

BE: Our sales department sells to manufacturing departments—so they're primarily engineers—technical people.

Ⓦ And what communication style do they usually fall into?

BE: Intellect style. So does that mean that if many of the individuals have an Intellect style, then the potential tone as an audience will be Intellect?

Ⓦ Yes—*exactly*. Now, the next w to find out about is *when,* when you will be speaking.

BE: What do I need to know about when? As long as I'm there on time, what difference does it make?

Ⓦ The when step is crucial because it signals you as to how many interest elements you need to integrate into your presentation to keep that audience listening.

BE: What do you mean by *interest elements?* I'm interesting, and I think my topic would automatically be interesting to our customers.

Ⓦ Maybe you are an interesting person, and I agree that customers should be interested in your topic. But the big question is—*were* they? Didn't some people leave, didn't you hear shuffling and conversations?

BE: I know I wasn't keeping their interest. But I thought by your description of Intellect audiences, they would listen to virtually anything—they listen to ideas and are not as visual as the other styles.

Ⓦ   But they're *human—I'm* an Intellect style and you put *me* to sleep.

BE: I thought you were supposed to be building my confidence.

Ⓦ   The point is, you must keep the *when* step in mind. For example, after a meal your audience tends, regardless of communication style, to nod off. Before a meal your audience may be focusing on their hunger pangs and not you. Therefore, if you are speaking when your audience is tired or hungry, you need to integrate visual aids—like the speaker before you did. Interesting stories or case studies that apply to your audience, appropriate humor, natural gestures and movement, all help you reach your goal—to keep that audience awake and with you. In the "Are You Interesting" chapter I will go into more depth on ways to get and keep audience interest.

BE: As usual, Wonder Word, your advice sounds great. I understand why the *when* step is so important. But how about the *where* step—that's next. It seems a little elementary. If I didn't know where I was speaking, how would I get there?

Ⓦ   No, no, Bob. The *where* step refers to the actual environment in which you'll be presenting. You need to find out the size and actual setup of the room. I remember one case I worked with who didn't pay attention to my expert guidance. She didn't find out where she would be speaking. This person had brought boards to use as visual aids. Unfortunately, the room had support pillars that blocked two–thirds of the audience's view. The visual aids were a crucial element in assisting the audience in understanding her presentation. Because the person didn't know the setup of the room beforehand, the likelihood for success was doomed from the start. If that speaker had only followed my advice, she could have rearranged the chairs to ensure that the audience could see the boards.

BE: The moral of the story seems to be that even the smallest detail can mean the difference between success and failure.

Ⓦ   That's right, Bob.

BE: My only concern is that I don't always have the time to go the day before to check out my setup. I don't think I'd trust someone's verbal description of a room. What do you recommend as an alternative?

(W) If you cannot go before the day of your presentation, get there early before anyone arrives. If you need to rearrange the setup, you'll have time to do that. If you need to use a microphone because of the room size, you'll have time to discover any idiosyncrasies that the microphone might have. Also, you'll have time to get comfortable with the area you'll be using.

BE: I guess that we just have the *what* step left to cover, Wonder Word.

(W) That's right, Bob—the last step in analyzing your audience is deciding what you will be speaking on and the viewpoint you want to represent. Regardless of the topic, the organization and language you use to present your message should vary according to the audience style. But, I'm getting ahead of myself. The next chapter will give you more specific information on that entire area.

BE: I'm exhausted, Wonder Word. I've already learned so much. I have only one concern now—there's so much to remember to do. How can I make sure I will take care of all the details that go into making a good audience analysis?

(W) I've made both of our jobs much easier. The next page is a checklist of all the items you could possibly need for a presentation. When you make your discovery phone calls, ask the individual in charge to provide the appropriate items. If you had filled a checklist out for the technicians' conference, what would you have included?

Review Bob's Audience Analysis–Public Speaking Checklist. Then when you must speak, use the blank checklist provided.

Audience Analysis and Speaking Engagement Checklist

Why were you asked to speak?

To inform customers about new products

Whom are you addressing?

Customers: Intellect audience

What is the size of the room you are speaking in?

Large — seats 300

When will you be speaking? (What time)

End of the day, 4:00 pm.

What is your underlying objective?

To sell customers on new products

What is the anticipated size of your audience?

100

What will be the set-up of chairs or tables?

Theatre style

Are there any obstacles inhibiting audience's vision of you?

No

Is there a lecturn?

Yes

Where is the location of the lecturn?

To the right, on the stage

Do you need a microphone? *Yes*   What type?

(Hand- or built-in with extension cord?; do you need extra mike cords?)

Do you need easels?

No

Do you need an overhead projector?

No

Do you need a slide carousel?

No

Where is your screen placed?

N/A

Do you need extra bulbs for equipment?

No

Do you need extra extension cords?

No

Do you need a pointer?

No

Are slides numbered?

N/A

Are overhead transparencies framed and numbered?

N/A

Where are sockets located?

Behind stage

Do you need a three-way plug or adaptor?

Yes, for microphone extension cord

Audience Analysis and Speaking Engagement Checklist

Why were you asked to speak?

Whom are you addressing?

What is the size of the room you are speaking in?

When will you be speaking? (What time)

What is your underlying objective?

What is the anticipated size of your audience?

What will be the set-up of chairs or tables?

Are there any obstacles inhibiting audience's vision of you?

Is there a lecturn?

Where is the location of the lecturn?

Do you need a microphone? What type?

Do you need easels?

Do you need an overhead projector?

Do you need a slide carousel?

Where is your screen placed?

Do you need extra bulbs for equipment?

Do you need extra extension cords?

Do you need a pointer?

Are slides numbered?

Are overhead transparencies framed and numbered?

Where are sockets located?

Do you need a three-way plug or adaptor?

Ⓦ Well, Bob, there's one final test before we move on to the next chapter. You're good at analyses, aren't you?

BE: I'm getting there. What new challenge do you have in mind?

Ⓦ The next page has a chart describing your audience at your last presentation. Based on the information listed, fill out the starred items. Then at the bottom, I'll fill in what your reasoning should have been in defining your audience style.

After reviewing Bob's choice and Wonder Word's rationale, fill out Case Study #2. Within each chapter we will request that you fill out additional items. When you have completed the book, the filled-in case studies will be a guideline for adapting your messages.

Bob's Case Study

Audience:	Users of product, usually technical engineers
Size:	100
Location:	Large room: seating capacity 300, set-up theatre style
Time of presentation:	4:00 p.m. (last speech of the day)
Topic:	Introduction of new product
Speaking order:	4th
Length of presentation:	½ hour

Given the above information, analyze the starred factors. Wonder Word's answer is at the bottom of the page.

★Style of audience:	*Intellect*
Type of language:	
Organization of message:	

Nonverbal elements:
★ clothing:
   gestures:
   movement:
	Neutral

Interest elements: type:	
Equipment needed:	
Your primary communication style:	

RATIONALE: The users were technical engineers. Most technical people tend to be intellects, thus the predominant audience style was intellect. As technicians, the group was not high powered, therefore neutral attire was most suitable.

Case Study #2—Charity Promotion

Audience:	Professionals, community leaders, executives
Size:	200
Location:	Hotel banquet room, set up with dinner tables, 10 people at each table
Time of presentation:	8:00 p.m. After dinner
Topic:	Promotion for a charity
Speaking order:	1st (The only speaker)
Length of presentation:	1 hour

Given the above information, analyze the starred factors, and then give your rationale for your answer at the bottom of the page. Turn to page 168 to check your answer.

★Style of audience:	
Type of language:	
Organization of message:	

Nonverbal elements:
★   clothing:
    gestures:
    movement:	

Interest elements: type:	
Equipment needed:	
Your primary communication style:	

RATIONALE:

Summary

When Bob Emerson arrived at the Technicians' conference, he was not prepared to deal with his surrounding environment. He was surprised to see an audience of 100 people. In his navy suit, he stood out among the casually dressed technicians. Failing to investigate in advance, he was not aware that he would be the fourth speaker and as he sat waiting, nervous panic began to build. Unfamiliar with the microphone, he felt embarrassment when it began to whine. These unnecessary occurrences could have been avoided through analyzing his audience. With the assistance of Wonder Word, Bob discovers the 5 W's of an audience analysis: WHO–WHY–WHEN–WHERE–and WHAT.

An audience analysis will assist you in determining how to present your message in the most effective manner.

- Determine *why* you've been asked to speak.
    Select appropriate topic.
    Identify secondary objective.
- Identify *who* your audience will be.
    Note characteristics of majority. (old/young, professional/nonprofessional, etc.)
    Determine styles of communication (audience's style/your style)
- Discover *when* you speak.
    Time of speech (after lunch, end of day, etc.)
    Order in which you speak (1st, 3rd, etc.)
    Select number and type of interest elements.
- Visit *location* where you will speak.
    Plan seating arrangement.
    Determine where to set up visual aids.
    Plan walking movements.
    Test equipment.
- Determine *what your message will be.*

By conducting an analysis of the audience, a speaker can predetermine the organization, language choice, clothing attire, and number and type of interest elements needed. Each of these elements and how to adapt these elements for various audiences are discussed in detail throughout the book.

As Bob discovered, an audience analysis is an essential part of every speech.

CHAPTER SIX

PREPARING THE PRESENTATION

Audience analysis is directed at answering the "Who", "Why", "Where", "When" and "What" of presentations. The next and perhaps most difficult question to answer is "How?". *How* to present your ideas as effectively and coherently as possible. *How* to organize the speech in order to capture and maintain audience interest and understanding. *How* to reinforce your main points and lead toward a call to action.

The "How?" is the organizational structure that provides a framework for the development of your ideas. It can be compared to the framework of a home. All further construction depends on a solid foundation. Decorating and finishing add color, vitality, and a personal touch to the structure. In a speech, the interest elements add a polished dimension to a presentation, but depend on a carefully-planned framework to be effective.

Ⓦ   Bob, it's time we discussed the most important element in a presentation—the organization. Only carefully–planned organization of your message can ensure clarity and understanding.

BE: As usual, Wonder Word, what you're saying makes sense, but doesn't the organization change according to the nature of the presentation?

Ⓦ   No. Although that's a common misunderstanding. Whether your objective is to inform, persuade, direct, sell, or entertain, the same basic structure can be applied. I invented this structure, and as you can imagine, I feel quite proud of it. I call it my *organizational matrix*. It has helped countless people over the years. Let's see what it can do for you, Bob.

In simplest form, it looks like this:

ORGANIZATIONAL MATRIX

I. INTRODUCTION
   A. Grabber
   B. Thesis

II. BODY
   A. Main points

III. CONCLUSION
   A. Review of thesis and main points
   B. Call to action
   C. Concluding grabber

BE: Really, Wonder Word—*introduction, body, conclusion*—there's nothing new about that. I thought you were going to give me a real solution to organizing my presentations.

Ⓦ You're right, Bob. It does seem elementary. But it's how people use or don't use this format that's important. The old theory of tell 'em what you're going to say, say it, and then tell 'em what you've said is the best way to reinforce your message so that your audience can remember. Let's examine the three main parts of my matrix to see how well your presentation followed my old hat guidelines.

BE: I was afraid of that. You do know how to get to the point, don't you, Wonder Word?

THE INTRODUCTION

An audience consciously and subconsciously judges a speaker during the first five minutes. The introduction, therefore, can either "make or break" the presentation, in that it sets the tone for what is to follow.

The introduction contains two main elements—the *grabber* and the *thesis.* The purpose of the grabber is to gain audience attention and establish rapport. By immediately capturing audience interest, a speaker can create positive expectations about the presentation. Since psychologists recognize that people hear what they expect to hear, initial positive expectations have an enormous impact on how an audience receives the ensuing information. By establishing rapport with an audience, the speaker increases his personal comfort level and bridges the gap between himself and the audience. Some common grabbers include:

1. Questions (rhetorical or requiring audience participation)
2. Jokes or humorous stories (relevant to the topic)
3. Quotations or historical illustrations of topic
4. References to current affairs or common items of interest
5. Use of space or gestures (enter or begin speaking from back of room; step down from podium)

6. Use of personal pronouns (I, you, we) to gain rapport
7. Use of contrasting or contradictory statements
8. Use of audio-visual aids as introduction to presentation

Ⓦ   Bob, would you say that you had an opening grabber?

BE: That's another trick I learned in my course. I always like to hear a good joke myself. This was one of my favorites, but the audience didn't seem to get it. It was all downhill from there.

Ⓦ   I understand, Bob. I enjoy a good joke myself. But tell me—do you often *tell* jokes?

BE: To be honest, I'd rather listen to them than tell them. I remember the punch line, but I don't like to spend all that time building up to the climax. I wish that my audience understood the joke before I finished telling it.

Ⓦ   That's your Driver personality showing, Bob. Two points I want to make: First, if you do use a joke as a grabber, make sure that it relates to the topic. Second, try using humor in different ways—an anecdote or amusing story or a funny one–liner rather than a staged joke. Look at the list of opening grabbers. How could you have gained audience interest without telling a joke?

Opening Grabbers

1. Question
   EX. ''When Horace Greeley invented this machine seventy years ago, could he have foreseen the major developments that have occurred in recent years?''
                          or
   ''How many of you here today have used motorized machinery for over five years? Ten years? Twenty years? How many have hoped that these machines would one day be computerized?''

2. Humor
   EX. ''Over the years, many of you have suggested changes in the design of our machines.'' (Pulls out long piece of paper, listing supposed requests; list is so long it reaches floor)

3. Quote or historical comments
    EX.   "America has long been known as the country of invention. Our ingenuity has kept us in the forefront of progress and economic stability. No product is ever final. Our research and development specialists continually work to refine and enhance. This computerized machinery is a result of such efforts at Watson, Inc."
4. Current affairs or common item of interest
    EX.   "This conference is as important to me as it is to you. It gives me an opportunity to get away from the sales staff who are marketing our new computerized machines, and the production force who makes them. It gives me an opportunity to talk with the people who *use* them, and that's the most important factor of all."
5. Use of gestures or space
    EX.   You would request a mike with an extension so that you could walk away from the podium and provide an interest element to stimulate attention from a tired audience.
6. Use of personal pronouns
    EX.   See above examples
7. Use of contrasting or contradictory statements
    EX.   "There are many of you who probably felt that our machines were on the way out. But, thanks to new technology and the continuous work of our research and development staff, our machines have been transformed into products of the future."
8. Use of visual aids
    EX.   Brief slide show depicting the physical changes in Watson, Inc.'s machines over the years, ending with focus on new computerized machinery.

ⓦ   How's that, Bob? Just a few examples to get you started.

BE: Wonder Word, you make it look so simple. I can't wait to get my second chance. Now, which grabber do you think I should use?

ⓦ   Slow down, Bob. That's just the opening. Let's continue with our discussion of organization before you make any final decisions. Also, don't forget that audience analysis is important in deciding the most appropriate introduction.

BE: Right! What's the next step, Wonder Word?

Ⓦ The grabber is the first part of the introduction, but another essential element is the thesis.

BE: I'm not sure what you mean—exactly what is the thesis in an introduction?

Ⓦ The *thesis* is the *raison d'être* of your presentation; the reason for its existence. It explains 1) Why you're there, and 2) Why the audience is there. Simple as it sounds, these two elements are commonly ignored in presentations.

The first part of a thesis is the clarification of the speaker's perspective on the topic. For example, the topic may be alternative sources of energy, but the speaker's perspective could be 1) that there are no reasonable alternative energy sources, or 2) that there are many resources, but they need further development before utilization, or 3) that there are abundant resources available now as alternative energy. This is just one indication of perspective. If the general topic were currently available alternative energy sources, the speaker's perspective could be 1) that he was in favor of developing them all, or 2) that he was in favor of utilizing a particular resource, or 3) that the best approach would be to keep these resources in reserve for future need. As you can see, the perspective identifies the speaker's specific viewpoint.

The second element in the thesis is the reason the audience should listen to you. You may be charming, intelligent, informed, enlightened, etc., but you still have to spell out for the audience exactly what they will get out of your presentation. Will they be more informed, motivated, better able to make a decision, entertained? What's in it for *them*? If you raise and answer this question, not only will your audience listen more carefully, but they also will assimilate and recall your message more accurately. Once again, telling them what you're going to say and why they should listen creates a positive environment where expectations will likely be reinforced and positively confirmed.

BE: I do believe I skipped the thesis entirely, Wonder Word. I told my joke, then went right into the various points I wanted to discuss.

Ⓦ I know, Bob. Many audiences have a difficult time following speakers who have never given overviews of what their presentations will entail.

BE: As a listener, that often happens to me. After five or ten minutes, I have no idea where the speaker is taking me, so I just watch.

Ⓦ And do you feel out of control when that happens?

BE: "Out of control, bored, and tuned out!

Ⓦ The two ways that an audience can experience control in a non–participatory situation are through (1) a clear overview of the topic and perspective, and (2) feedback.

BE: I know my audience will be better listeners if they feel in control. What would my thesis have been, Wonder Word?

Ⓦ Bob, I'm not here to give you all the answers. I'm here to guide you. You figure it out!

BE: Well, my perspective could be that the new computerized machines have surpassed our old line and our competitors' line through their new performance capabilities. And those technicians should listen to me because I can save them time and money if they come over to our new line.

Ⓦ A little rough, perhaps, but we'll save the polishing until later. That's the idea. Now shall we continue? The stage is set, so it's time to address the body of the presentation. The body of a presentation is composed of 1–5 main points. If there are more than 5 main points, your presentation becomes difficult to follow. (Alternative ways of delivering the information are recommended in this case. Choose a report or memo, or restrict your perspective so as to limit the number of main points.) The purpose of the main points is to provide evidence to substantiate your thesis. Each main point requires an interest element to maintain audience attention and reinforce the message. If you choose a verbal interest element such as a joke, story, analogy, or quotation, limit it to one per main point. Otherwise, your audience may become confused; some people may feel that you've gone on to a new topic; others may begin to realize that they missed the main point entirely. Other interest elements, such as gestures, walking patterns, and visual aids, will reinforce your main point in conjunction with a verbal interest element. How many main points did you have, Bob?

BE: Let's see. First, I talked about the history of our machines; then I reviewed the existing capabilities and limitations of the current line. (I love all that detail.) I then discussed how new technology has led to the development of the computerized machinery, and explained how this new product overcomes former limitations. Finally, I discussed potential future enhancements to computerization. Those are five main points, which fit right into your guidelines.

Ⓦ Did you forget everything I taught you about audience analysis?

BE: What do you mean, Wonder Word?

Ⓦ Since your presentation was late in the afternoon, do you think that factor should influence the number of main points?

BE: Late in the day, last presentation—I know the audience was tired. Do you think I should have limited the number of main points?

Ⓦ Would I have brought it up otherwise? Use only the most important points—there's no need to overload your audience.

BE: I see your point. Well, the most important information I wanted to bring up was (1) the existing capabilities and limitations of our old machines, (2) how our new technology has overcome these limitations, and (3) how these changes can benefit the user.

Ⓦ Now, that's better. I think even *I* could listen to that, though I never have been technically–minded.

BE: Thanks for the compliment. Maybe I should quit now while I'm ahead!

Ⓦ Are you going to leave your audience hanging there?

BE: I get the message—the conclusion, right?

Ⓦ Exactly. Brief, and to the point, but memorable. Here are the facts: There are three main elements in the conclusion: a *review* of the thesis and main points, a *call to action,* and a *concluding grabber*. The review is an opportunity to summarize your presentation. (This is the 'tell 'em what you told 'em' stage.) In summarizing, you can reinforce your main points through crystallizing your information. The call to action is the impetus to use the information presented. In the thesis, you've told the audience why they should listen. By requesting action from them, you are engaging them in active participation. They will also recall your message better if they have a way to use it. Speakers often overlook this step. Each time you speak, you can give the listener an opportunity to apply the information in some fashion. Do you want the audience to consider your opinion, report back to their supervisor/subordinates, elect you to office, buy your product, be aware of future developments, etc? *Tell* them what you want them to do.

The final step is to graciously conclude. In order to create a memorable impression, your last statements should be as interesting as your first. An excellent technique is to allude to your original grabber. By beginning and ending with the same reference, your presentation is neatly framed.

BE: I never thought about all those elements, Wonder Word. I used to just summarize and say "thanks"—a bit less dramatic than what you're suggesting.

Ⓦ Since I've given you a second chance, what will you say? What's your call to action?

BE: Since my objective is to persuade the users to implement our new machines, I'd better ask them to try it. Is that too bold?

Ⓦ You've given them good reasons to use your machines, haven't you? So ask them!

BE: My concluding grabber will depend on which opening grabber I choose. I'm going to fill out a complete matrix, Wonder Word, to get all my thoughts in order.

Ⓦ The matrix can help you even more, Bob. After you've written down your main ideas under each heading, select *key words* for each phrase. These key words can serve as simplified notes for your presentation. This reduced matrix format, plus any visual aids you may use, are all you need to make your presentation.

BE: But, you know me. If I don't have all my notes in front of me, I'll panic! I'll forget what I have to say! I'll blank out! Then what will I do?

(W)   Trust me, Bob. Too many notes cause confusion and create more anxiety about losing your place, dropping the notes, etc. Since I've given you a second chance, I'd like you to try it my way.

BE: Will you be there, Wonder Word?

(W)   YES, Bob.

BE: "And if I forget my place, you'll prompt me, right?"

(W)   I won't have to, Bob. You'll see . . . You'll see.

BE: One more question, though, Wonder Word. Back in the chapter on *Communicating Styles,* you mentioned two types of organization—recency and primacy. How can I work that element of organization into the matrix framework?

(W)   Good point, Bob. I almost forgot to tie that in. If your audience is primarily Driver or Intellect, they like to hear information in the primacy mode. Your thesis should be direct, and to the point. For example, if quarterly earnings were up 3.5 million dollars, your thesis could be "Careful Management has produced a quarterly gain of $3.5 million. Supporting main points could include 1) How a strike was averted, 2) How shipments of raw materials were on target with production requirements, and 3) How generally successful the new product line was. If the audience is primarily Amiable or Passive, such a direct approach could overwhelm them. To accommodate their listening needs, you could use the recency mode by changing the thesis to a "review of management decisions in the last quarter." After you review the main points, you could summarize by indicating that careful management has contributed to a quarterly gain of $3.5 million. Another factor to consider is the nature of your information—good news (positive) or bad news (negative). If your company had lost $3.5 million in the last quarter, even with an audience of Intellect–Drivers, it would not be good policy to deliver that news item first. Adopt the recency mode. For example, the thesis could be "A Review of Several Factors that Affected Production This Quarter." After you demonstrate that 1) the strike you had expected to be over by May continued into October, 2) Your company experienced unprecedented shipping delays of raw materials, and 3) The new product line had to be recalled, you conclude by stating that considering all of these circumstances, your company was fortunate to lose only $3.5 million.

BE: You sure are the clever one when it comes to words. Guess that's how you got your name.

Ⓦ Speaking of words, this is a good time to decide what type of language to choose for your particular audience. Since you've examined your thesis, objectives, and main points, and you are aware of your audience style (Intellect), what type of language should you use?

BE: Well, I know I should use technical language because we both understand the terminology. And because the audience is primarily Intellect, I should use precise terms and detailed descriptions. What else?

Ⓦ If your goal is to persuade them to use your product, your language should also be forceful. Avoid tentative terms. You need to convince them that your product is the best on the market. Now, what was the secondary style of your audience?

BE: Amiable. They were casual, wore short–sleeved shirts, corduroys, etc. In terms of language choice, I should use informal language rather than formal, and make personal references when appropriate.

Ⓦ Excellent, Bob. You've adopted both your language and organization to your audience of users.

BE: After I fill out the matrix, Wonder Word, I'll prepare my notes for the presentation.

Ⓦ One more thing before you fill out your matrix, Bob. Let's return to your case study to make sure you've followed everything we've discussed in the chapter.

Review Bob's choices and Wonder Word's rationale on the case study before filling out Case Study #2.

Then review the matrix Bob filled out. On the next page, he translated his ideas to *key words*.

Compare the two. Instructions will follow.

Bob's Case Study

Audience:	Users of product, usually technical engineers
Size:	100
Location:	Large room: seating capacity 300, set up theatre style
Time of presentation:	4:00 p.m. (last speech of the day)
Topic:	Introduction of new product
Speaking order:	4th
Length of presentation:	½ hour

Given the above information, analyze the starred factors. Wonder Word's answer is at the bottom of the page.

★Style of audience:	*Intellect*
★Type of language:	*Multi-syllabic words; specific, technical terms*
★Organization of message:	*Primacy*

Nonverbal elements:
★   clothing:
    gestures:
    movement:
	Neutral

Interest elements: type:	
Equipment needed:	
Your primary communication style:	

RATIONALE: The users were technical engineers. Most technical people tend to be Intellects; thus, the predominant audience style was Intellect. As technicians, the group was not high powered, therefore neutral attire was most suitable. Intellects use multi-syllabic and specific, technical language. They relate well to those who use similar language patterns. They also prefer to hear their messages delivered in a primacy mode, which is their method of organizing messages.

Case Study #2 — Charity Promotion

Audience:	Professionals, community leaders, executives
Size:	200
Location:	Hotel banquet room, set up with dinner tables, 10 people at each table
Time of presentation:	8:00 p.m. After dinner
Topic:	Promotion for a charity
Speaking order:	1st (The only speaker)
Length of presentation:	1 hour

Given the above information, analyze the starred factors, and then give your rationale for your answer at the bottom of the page. Turn to page 168 to check your answer.

★ Style of audience:	
★ Type of language:	
★ Organization of message:	
Nonverbal elements: ★ clothing: gestures: movement:	
Interest elements: type:	
Equipment needed:	
Your primary communication style:	

RATIONALE:

Organizational Matrix Fill-In Sheet

I. INTRODUCTION
A. Grabber
How many of you here today have used motorized machinery for over 5 years? 10 years? 20 years? How many have hoped that these machines would one day be computerized?
B. Thesis Statement
1. Perspective:
Our new computerized machines have surpassed current performance capabilities of motorized machines and competitors' models.
2. Importance:
Users can save time and money if they switch to this new line.

II. BODY
A. Main Point (Interest Element)
Existing capabilities and limitations of the motorized machines.
1. Interfaces with 675 series only
2. Allows for no new enhancements
B. Main Point (Interest Element)
New technology has overcome these limitations
1. Interfaces with entire line 800 series down.
2. New enhancements can be added.
C. Main Point (Interest Element)
How these changes benefit the user
1. Need to stock only one line of machines; less inventory means less cost.
2. Future enhancements build off one element which reduces potential for error.

III. CONCLUSION
A. Review of main points and thesis
Computerized machines outperform others because of
a.
b.
c.
B. Call to action
Make technical preparations for switching over to this computerized line.
C. Concluding grabber
Because our machines are computerized, you will be able to use them for five, ten, twenty or more years—a product of the future as well as the present.

Key Words Matrix Fill-In Sheet

I. INTRODUCTION
   A. Grabber
      How long used motorized machines?
      Hope computerized?
   B. Thesis Statement
      1. Perspective:
         Comp. Machines surpassed capabilities
      2. Importance:
         Save $, time

II. BODY
   A. Main Point (Interest Element)
      Existing cap. & limit.
   B. Main Point (Interest Element)
      New Technology
   C. Main Point (Interest Element)
      Benefits

III. Conclusion
   A. Review of Main Points and Thesis
      C. M. OUTPERFORMS
   B. Call to Action
      PREPARE TO SWITCH
   C. Concluding Grabber
      USE FOR NEXT X # YEARS

Now it's your turn. Choose a sample presentation topic that you will develop during the following chapters. Fill out the Organizational Matrix, then a Key Words Matrix.

Organizational Matrix Fill-In Sheet

I. INTRODUCTION
   A. Grabber

   B. Thesis Statement
      1. Perspective:

      2. Importance:

II. BODY
   A. Main Point (Interest Element)

   B. Main Point (Interest Element)

   C. Main Point (Interest Element)

III. CONCLUSION
   A. Review of Main Points and Thesis

   B. Call to Action

   C. Concluding Grabber

Key Words Matrix Fill-In Sheet

I. INTRODUCTION
   A. Grabber

   B. Thesis Statement
      1. Perspective:

      2. Importance:

II. BODY
   A. Main Point (Interest Element)

   B. Main Point (Interest Element)

   C. Main Point (Interest Element)

III. CONCLUSION
   A. Review of Main Points and Thesis

   B. Call to Action

   C. Concluding Grabber

Summary

Although Bob understood that every presentation was composed of an introduction, body, and conclusion, he did not realize the purpose of each element in the organizational process. He started with a joke because he thought you should *always* begin in that fashion. Overlooking the thesis, Bob went right into his five main points. Then at the end of his talk, he simply thanked the audience for their time and attention. Since he had not provided his audience with an overview, perspective, or reason to listen, it is unlikely that many of them actually heard his message. And because his opening and closing were uninteresting and ordinary, they were undoubtedly forgotten along with the rest of the information.

When Bob was persuaded to apply his ideas to the organizational matrix, he discovered that he produced a concise, dynamic, logical structure which provided both organizational clarity and the key words from which he could speak. To reinforce the importance and purpose of each element of the presentation, let's review the introduction, body, and conclusion.

Wonder Word's Organizational Matrix

I. INTRODUCTION
   A. Grabber
      1. Gain attention
      2. Establish rapport
   B. Thesis
      1. Introduce your perspective of topic
      2. Give audience reason to listen

II. BODY
   A. Main Point with Interest Element
      1. Provide evidence to substantiate thesis
      2. Limit to insure clarity
         4–5 main points
         (One verbal interest element per main point)

III. CONCLUSION
   A. Review of Main Points and Thesis
      1. Reinforce main ideas
      2. Summarize presentation
   B. Call to Action
      1. Give audience method to use information
      2. Encourage active participation
   C. Concluding Grabber
      1. Create memorable impression
      2. Frame the presentation

CHAPTER SEVEN

ARE YOU INTERESTING?

At mid-point in your speech, your eyes wander through the audience. Two men are talking to each other in the back row, a young woman has taken out her knitting, another appears to be trying desperately to keep her chin from falling to her chest, and immediately in front of you, someone has the gall to yawn. In view of this disinterest, your need to recapture their attention is of immediate concern. Before going on to the next point, you decide to tell a good joke, thinking, "That will wake them up." It falls flat! "Now what am I going to do?" you wonder as you search for a new starting point. In your panic you see a young man smiling up at you with encouragement. That one smile gets you through. As you leave, you wonder, "How could I have kept *everyone's* attention?"

It takes more than a good joke to answer the question "are you interesting?" with a "Yes." From the opening grabber to the concluding statement, your speech must contain elements that will broaden its appeal. To assist you in keeping an audience involved and alive, this chapter is devoted to the various types of interest elements. They include vocal quality, stories, humor, analogies, quotations, visual aids and movement. Without the use of interest elements, a large percentage of your audience will tune out the entire verbal message. Interest elements, therefore, are *key* in eliminating this potential barrier.

One of the most frequently neglected interest elements is *vocal quality*. Varied pitch, rate, and volume levels are necessary to communicate in a conversational manner. In your interpersonal conversations, your voice rises and falls naturally. A monotone voice inevitably wins the blue ribbon for boredom.

Vocal quality is also important in the delivery of *humor* and *stories*—two other key interest elements. Humor is one of the best ways to break the ice with your audience; however, it must be delivered appropriately to be effective. Before humor is used, determine whether it complements your natural style, and whether it is appropriate for your audience. Humor and stories should pertain to the topic of your speech.

Analogies, quotations and visual aids are commonly used as interest elements. Analogies are effective to convey abstract ideas in a concrete fashion. Quotations, when used, should be from an established source and stated accurately. The use of visual aids, such as films, charts, and slides, stimulates both the visual and auditory senses. Appealing to more than one sense has advantages: interest is enhanced, information is retained longer, and understanding is improved.

On a nonverbal level, *movement* is a primary element of interest. Gestures and walking add vitality to a presentation; but plan gestures and walking patterns carefully to avoid distracting from your verbal message.

If you have always believed that you were innately interesting, yet find your audiences getting bored, falling asleep or, worse yet, getting up to leave, incorporation of these interest elements into your speeches will teach you the lesson that Bob had to learn from Wonder Word.

BE: "Wonder Word, I don't see how adding gestures and some stories to my presentation will transform me into a dynamic, spellbinding speaker."

Ⓦ "You'll see, Bob. We'll transform your dull presentations into interesting ones—ones that the audience wants to listen to—ones where the audience won't have to mentally work too hard to get the main ideas. Your presentations will fit the audience's *needs* or *expectations,* entertain them, and compel them into action!"

BE: Whoa! I'm not the least bit interested in becoming a professional public speaker. I'm just Bob Emerson, an average executive on the climb up the proverbial corporate ladder—the guy who hates to stand up before an audience and make a fool of himself.

Ⓦ Bob, we've already established your desire to maintain a professional image. However, boring your audience makes you appear foolish as well.

BE: But I tried a joke and it didn't work. Isn't humor part of being interesting to your audience?

Ⓦ Yes, Bob, but remember what we determined in the last chapter—that you are not a natural joke teller. Thus the rhetorical questions we selected for your opening grabber are much better suited to your style, your topic, and the style of your audience.

BE: What type of interest elements would I use with other audiences? I'm not always presenting to Intellects.

Ⓦ An excellent question! Drivers enjoy displays, so visual interest elements, such as slides, would be appealing. Passive audiences would accept quotations if from acknowledged and recognizable sources. Amiables, as you well know, enjoy stories and humor. Actually, almost all of the interest elements can be used with each audience type if language and delivery style are presented in a compatible fashion. Remember, Bob, people, as they listen, need to be able to visualize what you are talking about, and a good way to do that is to apply the information to *them*. For example, because your audience was made up primarily of customers, you could have related stories or examples of special customers in the audience who use your existing products to explain how the new product would assist or benefit them in the future. This technique would paint a clear picture for them as to why they should listen, and involve them in your presentation at the same time.

BE: I get the picture—like what you just did for me—relating your main points to something personal. I can't wait to recreate my presentation. I can think of countless case studies that an Intellect audience would enjoy. I can even think of several analogies that would be perfect for my talk.

Ⓦ You'd better slow down, Bob. Let's not go beyond reason. In any presentation, you should never have more than *one* verbal interest element per main point. A series of stories or any combination of the various verbal interest elements will only confuse the audience.

BE: That makes a lot of sense.

Ⓦ Bob, *everything* I say makes a lot of sense. Now, I still need to expand on how you use quotations and analogies. Let's look at a few more examples. Quotations are useful when your goal is to prove a point; refer to statements made by an established expert. For example, a quote on public speaking:
Let us have a reason for beginning, and let our end be within due limits. For a speech that is wearisome only stirs up anger.
Saint Ambrose

BE: Who wouldn't agree with that!

Ⓦ Analogies are good visualizers. If you are delivering abstract or complex concepts, compare your point with something the audience is *aware* of—compare the unknown with the known. For example: The taste of peppermint patties is like a cool breeze on a hot summer day.

BE: I'm catching on—I'm turning on the television for the audience and I'm doing it through what I'm saying.

(W) Interesting analogy! You're on target with your comment that presentations should be along the same lines as a television program. And as with television, there's more than the verbal message; there's also *how you say it* and what you are physically doing while you are saying it all. Because audiences react to visual and paralinguistic stimuli significantly faster than they do to verbal stimuli, what you do as a public speaker can either *underscore* your verbal message or create a *barrier* to your audience's reception of your verbal message.

BE: Are you suggesting that I should stand still and deliver my message so I don't interfere with my points?

(W) No, I'm not suggesting that at all. If you stood perfectly still, you'd have to have the voice and delivery style of a Richard Burton to rivet home your points. Since you don't have that advantage, you need to choreograph gestures and movement into your presentation. Again, your goal is to help your audience *hear* your message and *keep* their attention. The key, Bob, is that you need to be appropriate and adapt your visual interest elements to assist your various audiences to hear your messages. For your Driver and Amiable audiences, interest is maintained through frequent movement and defined gestures that underscore or illustrate your verbal message. For your Passive and Intellect audiences, limit movement and use succinct but fewer gestures. For example, walk into Driver and Amiable audiences. However, with Passive and Intellect audiences, just move to the side of the podium. To demonstrate a gesture that underscores a verbal message, consider the following:

Phrase	Gesture
"Over the past two years we've experienced significant growth."	Make your hand gesture move from a low point to a high point with the palm down.
"I don't understand why this happened."	Shake your head slightly from side to side while raising your shoulders.
"I have given you all of the information you need."	Extend one or both arms with palms up toward the listeners.

BE: So in my speech, I can use a story, limited movement and analogies to maintain the interest of my audience. Right, Wonder Word?

Ⓦ   Right, Bob.

As Bob has done, review all of the interest elements and select those that would be appropriate for your presentation. Consider your natural style, topic, and audience. Also, complete the interest element section on the case studies.

Bob's Case Study

Audience:	Users of product, usually technical engineers
Size:	100
Location:	Large room: seating capacity 300, set-up, theatre style
Time of presentation:	4:00 p.m. (last speech of the day)
Topic:	Introduction of new product
Speaking order:	4th
Length of presentation:	½ hour

Given the above information, analyze the starred factors. Wonder Word's answer is at the bottom of the page.

★Style of audience:	*Intellect*
★Type of language:	*Multi-syllabic words; specific, technical terms*
★Organization of message:	*Primacy*
Nonverbal elements: ★ clothing: ★ gestures: ★ movement:	*Neutral* *A few, small, illustrative gestures* *Don't move into audience, stay behind podium or move next to podium*
★Interest elements: type:	*Stories regarding product, analogies*
Equipment needed:	
Your primary communication style:	

RATIONALE: The users were technical engineers. Most technical people tend to be Intellects, thus the predominant audience style was Intellect. As technicians, the group was not high powered, therefore neutral attire was most suitable. Intellects use multi-syllabic and specific, technical language. They relate well to those who use similar language patterns.

RATIONALE *(continued)*:
They also prefer to hear their messages delivered in a primacy mode that is their method of organizing messages. After three speakers, any group will begin to fatigue. To maintain interest, a variety as well as quantity of interest elements are needed. Gestures will add some interest but must be small and illustrative to avoid distracting the Intellect style. Intellects prefer distance; thus, movement should be limited to the area around the podium. Humor was omitted due to difficulty of selection for an Intellect audience. Stories were related specifically to the product because Intellects become impatient with personal experiences of the speaker. Analogies could have added another interest dimension without creating a barrier for the Intellect audience.

Case Study # 2—Charity Promotion

Audience:	Professionals, community leaders, executives
Size:	200
Location:	Hotel banquet room, set up with dinner tables, 10 people at each table
Time of presentation:	8:00 p.m. After dinner
Topic:	Promotion for a charity
Speaking order:	1st (The only speaker)
Length of presentation:	1 hour

Given the above information, analyze the starred factors, and then give your rationale for your answer at the bottom of the page. Turn to page 168 to check your answer.

★Style of audience:	
★Type of language:	
★Organization of message:	
Nonverbal elements: ★ clothing: ★ gestures: ★ movement:	
★Interest elements: type:	
Equipment needed:	
Your primary communication style:	

RATIONALE:

Summary

Your audience will find it difficult to remain alert, attentive and involved without the use of interest elements. The various types of interest elements include vocal quality, stories, humor, analogies, quotations, visual aids, gestures, and movement. They assist your audience in listening to the entire message and also provide a means for improving understanding.

The interest elements you can use are:

- Vocal Quality
    Vary pitch, rate, and loudness
    Establish conversational manner
- Humor
    Analyze your natural style
    Consider appeal to audience
- Stories
    Select to pertain to topic
    Limit length
- Analogies
    Use to convey abstract ideas
    Select those that are readily understood
- Quotations
    State accurately
    Select from an established source
- Visual Aids
    Determine type based on audience size
    (See Chapter 8)
- Gestures
    Use to underscore message
    Use to illustrate your words/points
- Walking Pattern
    Choreograph with verbal message
    Choreograph movement according to audience

To determine which of the interest elements to select, consider your natural style. (If you have never successfully delivered a punch line, then omit humor from your speech.) Also consider what would appeal to your audience. An Intellect audience, for example, would be responsive to analogies, while an Amiable audience relates well to stories. The amount of movement used is also dependent upon your audience. Move into Amiable or Driver audiences, but limit movement with Passive or Intellect audiences.

The number of interest elements you select depends upon when you speak. When faced with adverse conditions such as speaking immediately after lunch to a full and content audience, or after three other speakers, an increased number of interest elements is needed. It is recommended, however, that you not exceed one verbal interest element for every main point in your speech.

To convey enthusiasm, vary vocal quality. To stimulate more than one sense, use visual aids. To add vitality to your presentation, use movement. All of the interest elements are relevant when you want to answer "yes" to the question *Are you interesting?*

CHAPTER EIGHT

WHAT'S SO GOOD ABOUT VISUAL AIDS?

Have you ever thought of the reasons why you use visual aids during a presentation? If you don't use them, have you considered why not? The following may be among your possible responses:

1. "I don't use visual aids because they are too gimmicky."
2. "I do use visual aids, but only as a crutch for recalling information."
3. "I am afraid to use visual aids because, in order to be effective, they require a certain amount of expertise."

If any of the above statements express your feelings about visual aids, then increased knowledge of their function and use may change your view.

Consider visual aids as viable interest elements, and also as a means for conveying or reinforcing your verbal message. As Wonder Word might say, "One picture is worth ten thousand words." One picture on a graph *can* easily convey an idea that would be cumbersome to explain with words. Look at the following example. Which way is easier to describe the directions to Speechville Road—verbally or graphically?

If you are coming from Flopland, take Route One E until you come to the rotary. At the rotary, do not veer off onto Stray Rd., but continue around, taking Route One N. Take exit 47 off Route One N. Stay to the right and exit onto Nervous Lane S. Three miles down Nervous Lane you'll come to an intersection where Control Circle crosses Nervous Lane. When you cross this intersection, Nervous Lane changes to Calm Street because you are now in Skillciti. Continue south on Calm Street for approximately 1½ miles where Control Circle again crosses Calm Street. Take a left turn onto Control Circle, go down 3 miles and you will see Speechville Road. Turn right onto Speechville Road and #30 is the third building on your right.

If you are coming from Praktiss Town, then you can take either Nervous Lane S or Anxiety Road. Nervous Lane S . . .

Undoubtedly, the map is a much easier and clearer display of the route. With this type of information, it would even be difficult to remember the route without taking notes. Visualization is a positive advantage. Throughout this chapter the important reasons for using visual aids and the ways to use them most effectively will be discussed. The various types of visual aids include chalkboards, overhead transparencies, slides, boards, flipcharts, and films.

FLOPLAND

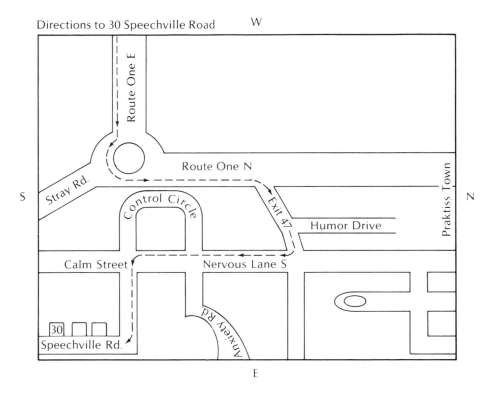

Directions to 30 Speechville Road

Skillciti

⊢———⊣
1 mile

There are four basic advantages for using visual aids during a presentation:

1. They increase the speed at which your message is received. The reason for this is that the nerve from the eye (ocular nerve) travels a shorter distance to the brain than the auditory nerve.
2. Visual aids improve understanding of your message. With all of the idiosyncracies in our language, listeners can give your message a variety of interpretations, and not necessarily the meaning you intend. However, if you present for your listeners a visual image of the meaning you want to convey, they will adopt your interpretation.

3. Visual aids enhance the retention of your message. According to research, if your message is received through words alone, only up to 10 percent of your message will be subject to recall one week later; but if verbal and visual messages are presented simultaneously, up to 65 percent of your message will be retained one week later.

4. Visual aids are interesting and add to the flow of your presentation.

To maximize the advantages that visual aids provide, select the type of visual aid you use based on (1) the purpose of your presentation, (2) your audience style, and (3) the size of your audience.

If your goal is to entertain, then slides, boards, or flipcharts are your best vehicles. Slides are most effective.

If you wish to impress your audience, a multi-image slide presentation is your best choice. Professionally prepared boards or handouts also work well.

If your objective is to persuade, then boards, slides, overhead transparencies, or handouts should be your choice.

If your aim is to inform, use flipcharts, chalkboards, overhead transparencies, boards, or handouts.

Once you have identified your purpose, consider the type of audience you will address: Driver, Passive, Amiable or Intellect. Virtually any of the visual aids can be used with each audience, but the rationale for use and the design of the visuals will differ. Your energetic, Driver audiences can appreciate flashy multi-colored slides, or overheads and slides using the revelation technique (which will be explained later.) For Intellect audiences, select a visual display of uncluttered information. Charts, slides, or overheads can be effective. With Intellect audiences, where the information may be technical, visual diagrams can be extremely useful. Amiables would appreciate illustrative drawings on flipcharts, boards or slides. Select pictures rather than graphs. With Passive audiences, any type of visual aid can be used to clarify or reinforce main points. Avoid use of flashy displays.

Another influential factor in the selection of visual aids is the audience size. Don't make the mistake of arriving to your destination faced with an audience of 150 people and with charts only large enough to be viewed by those sitting in the front two rows. When speaking before an audience of one to fifty people, you may choose to use boards, flip-charts, chalkboards, overhead transparencies, or slides. When your audience is fifty to one hundred people, use large boards, overhead transparencies or slides. For an audience of over one hundred people, use slides.

In addition to selecting visual aids that are not appropriate to audience size, another common mistake is to overload visuals with too much information. Each visual should convey only one main point. Also, there should be no more than seven lines of copy and no more than five words per line.

When illustrating a main concept that involves more than one point, use the *revelation* technique. With this technique you begin by covering all but one point. Reveal each following point as you refer to it. You may use a piece of paper as a cover during your presentation or attach lifting overlays when developing your visual.

The *evolution* technique is to be used with transparencies or slides.

When using transparencies, develop a series of overlays. The base transparency will have your first point printed or illustrated on it. Then each following point will be placed on a different overlay (varying colors for each point is recommended for added design and interest). As you present each point, flip over the appropriate overlay.

When using slides in the evolution technique, the first slide is made with only your first point on it. One point is then added to each following slide. The point that you are referring to at the time should be in a different color than the others. This indicates where the attention of your listeners should be.

Example of Evolution Technique

Advantages of Visual Aids	Advantages of Visual Aids	Advantages of Visual Aids
Messages are:	Messages are:	Messages are:
1. Received more quickly	1. Received more quickly 2. Retained longer	1. Received more quickly 2. Retained longer 3. Understood more clearly

Do not wait until the time of your presentation to determine whether or not everything is in the proper order and flows smoothly. Practice with your visual aid as you practice your speech. However, if a mistake does occur during your speech, respond calmly, correct the mistake quickly, and continue with your presentation. Do not draw undue attention to your mistake. If necessary, continue on with your presentation without the use of your visual aid. Always practice your speech without your visual aid in the event that a mishap does occur. Think of visual accompaniment as only a *supplement* to your verbal message.

Bob thought that he could give an interesting speech *without* visual aids. Let's tune in as Wonder Word tries to convince him to use visual aids.

Ⓦ   Bob, I think I've given you enough basic information about visual aids. Now let's see how we can integrate visual accompaniment into your presentation.

BE: Wait, just wait a minute. First you've got me reorganizing my speech; then you have me gesturing and walking like an actor on stage, and now you want me to worry about visual aids, too. Instead of reducing my concerns I'm going to be paralyzed by indecision. I'll be so confused—walk on this phrase, gesture there, raise my arm here, move to the left three steps—and now you want me to use visual aids. Wonder Word, I just wanted some basic ideas on how to be more interesting and effective as a speaker. You're trying to drive me from being an amateur to being a professional."

Ⓦ   Bob, I don't want to turn you into a professional presenter; I just want to make your presentations more professional. Visual aids actually assist you in organizing your message and staying on the right track. When we're finished, I guarantee you'll see that by using visual aids, your job as a presenter will be easier—much easier. Let's begin by analyzing your presentation and audience.

Let's see what types of visual aids would have been appropriate for 100 people.

Type of Visual Aid	Size of Audience		
	1–50	50–100	101 +
Chalkboards	x		
Overhead transparencies	x	x	
Slides	x	x	x
Boards	x	x	
Flipcharts	x		

Ⓦ   See, Bob? You could use boards, slides, or overhead transparencies.

As Bob considers the possibilities, Wonder Word continues.

Ⓦ   Which of these have you had experience with?

BE: I've used slides and the overhead projector.

Ⓦ   Have you ever had any training in their use?

BE: No, of course not. They're easy enough; I just tell our art department what I want and they design them, or I use our photo machine and make my own overheads.

Ⓦ   Have you ever found that what your art department thinks is important is not what *you* think is important?

BE: I don't understand what you're getting at.

Ⓦ   Have the slides they developed for you always communicated the messages you wanted them to?

BE: For the most part, but every now and then I don't know what the slides mean. Several times I've gotten the slides back and couldn't figure out how to use them.

Ⓦ   You'll find, Bob, that many people have experienced the same thing. I'm not saying that the art department isn't doing its job, but they can't climb into your mind and interpret what you want to communicate to your various audiences. Therefore, I recommend that you create your own story boards (rough sketches) for the slides. Then they will say exactly what you want them to say. Then give those roughs to the art department so they can transform them into professional slides.

BE: But I'm not an artist.

Ⓦ   And your art department professionals are not mind readers. When you tell the art department what you want for slides, do you ever work with an illustrator to complete the slides?

BE: Of course not—I'm busy—I expect them to know . . .

Ⓦ   You *expect!* You can't expect someone else to interpret your messages. Only *you* know what's important. Therefore, you ought to be doing the initial development.

BE: Wonder Word, are you trying to tell me that I should have used slides for my presentation?

Ⓦ No, not necessarily. My purpose right now is to discover what visual accompaniment you have used in the past and how you've prepared them. What about overheads—tell me what you do with them.

BE: Let me see . . . I've used them for meetings. I usually take pages of my reports and have them transferred onto a transparency and speak from that.

Ⓦ First of all, if you do that there is likely to be too much information per page. Remember, no more than seven lines. Secondly, have you found that people in the back tend to squint at your overheads?

BE: I never noticed.

Ⓦ When you are speaking in your meetings, how long do you actually use the overhead?

BE: I usually use them throughout my entire talk.

Ⓦ And how long is that?

BE: Oh, anywhere from twenty minutes to an hour.

Ⓦ Have any of your meeting attendees ever complained of *headaches?*

BE: Sure, that's a standing joke at all our meetings—most everyone brings a personal bottle of aspirin.

Ⓦ Are *all* your meetings that intense?

BE: Some of them—I think it's now more of a tradition.

Ⓦ Are you aware that the light in the overhead projector gives people headaches? The intensity of the light affects the viewers' eyes. I recommend turning the machine off when it's not in use, or you can place a blank form over it when you are not referring to it.

BE: That's important to know. I'll definitely limit my use of overheads. Maybe I should eliminate their use altogether.

Ⓦ No, they have a place, Bob. I'll go into more detail about overheads and slides later in this chapter. Now, let's focus on your presentation. Which type of visual medium would you like to use in your second chance?

BE: Hmmm . . . not the overhead, not formal enough.

Ⓦ Good.

BE: Not the flip chart, also too informal.

Ⓦ Right.

BE: Not boards, I've never used them before. I guess I'd choose slides. The first thing I'd do is decide on what I'd want on them, then I'd take them to the art department and go over everything with an artist. How does that sound?

Ⓦ Not bad, Bob. Let's discuss this a little more. What did the speaker before you use?

BE: Slides—and it was a very clear presentation.

Ⓦ Have you ever eaten too much of your favorite food?

BE: I don't see how this applies, Wonder Word.

Ⓦ Do you think one-and-a-half hours of low lights and slides on a screen could get old?

BE: Too much of a good thing, eh? I should use another visual medium to make me stand out in the audience's mind. Plus, that gives them an opportunity to look at something besides the screen.

Ⓦ What do you think you could use instead of slides?

BE: Boards—but because I've never used them, I'd feel uncomfortable.

Ⓦ We'll assess your presentation and decide where boards would be appropriate. Then we'll discuss what they would say. Finally, I will coach you on how to use the boards. During your presentation you mention a new product. A visual display of the new Watson machine would have given your audience a picture, and would have also assisted you in describing the dimensions of the machine. Intellects would want to know how much office space it will take.

Also, the benefits of the machine and a graph of its various functions would have assisted you in recalling your main points without reading your notes. Most importantly, it would help your audience remember these important points.

BE: I can see how those boards would highlight my presentation. But using boards requires a certain amount of skill, doesn't it? What techniques will make me appear more polished?

Ⓦ When using a board, (1) Point to the visual with the hand closest to it. This keeps your body open to the audience. (2) Be careful to move eye contact from the visual back to your audience within three seconds so that you are able to maintain control and rapport. (3) When you are not referring to the visual, cover it with a blank board or stand in front of the visual. (4) If you must refer to a visual for a second time, and you have already used it previously, make a duplicate visual. (5) In developing your message, pause verbally while moving the board, flipping the chart, or writing on the chalkboard or flipchart. This will guarantee that your entire verbal message is heard by your audience.

In the future, Bob, when boards are not appropriate, review this information regarding the other types of visual aids.   When using an overhead transparency, (1) Create a border on the machine with masking tape. This will insure that the transparency is sitting straight on the machine. (2) Prepare a blank transparency to be used when there is a pause between transparencies. (3) Use a pointer to refer your audience to each point on the visual. A pencil point may be used to point on the transparency, or a long pointer may be used to point to the screen. (4) Be sure to remain out of the light of the overhead and number each transparency to make certain that they are kept in order.

If you decide to use slides as your visual, (1) Have them prepared professionally. (2) Have blank slides made for long transition statements that do not require visualization. (3) Be sure to know the content of each slide. This will enable you to maintain eye contact with your audience instead of looking back and forth between the slides and your audience. (4) Have a listing of slides before you for reference. (5) If you are using rear projection, develop and follow a script. Illustrate each slide on the corresponding section of the script. Give a duplicate to the person operating the projector.

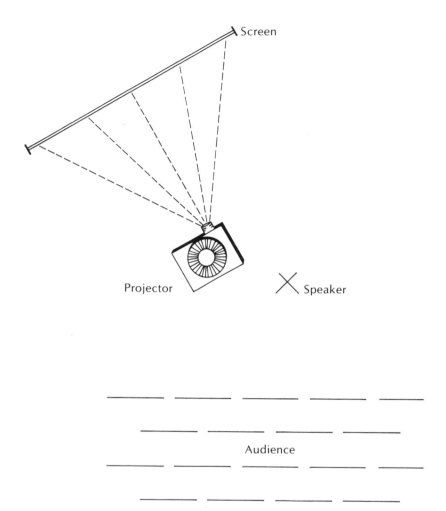

Proper positioning for an overhead or front projection slide show presentation.

And practice with the projection operator. (6) When operating the projector yourself, hold the advance mechanism behind your back or place on the lecturn, if available. (7) Use a long pointer to refer your audience to specific points on the slide. Point to the screen, but be sure to remain out of the projector light.

Ⓦ The most important element in setting up your visual aid is to make certain that everyone in your audience has a clear view of the entire visual. This is best accomplished by placing your easel or screen in

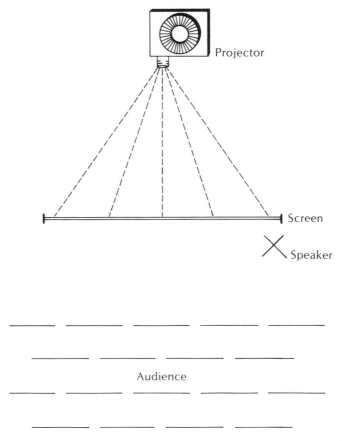

Proper positioning for a rear projection slide show presentation.

the corner of the room. However, if you are using rear projection for a slide presentation, the equipment requires that the screen be placed in the center of the room.

BE: Wonder Word, with all of this information, I can't fail.

ⓦ   Yes, you can, Bob, unless you *practice.* Practice with your speech so it flows without disruption while you're trying to figure out whether or not it's time to go on to the next board.

Bob is continuing to fill out his case study. You should be following his lead. Review Bob's choices and Wonder Word's answer; then fill out the second case study. Don't forget to list your reasons.

Bob's Case Study

Audience:	Users of product, usually technical engineers
Size:	100
Location:	Large room: seating capacity 300, set-up theatre style
Time of presentation:	4:00 p.m. (last speech of the day)
Topic:	Introduction of new product
Speaking order:	4th
Length of presentation	½ hour

Given the above information, analyze the starred factors. Wonder Word's answer is at the bottom of the page.

★ Style of audience:	*Intellect*
★ Type of language:	*Multi-syllabic words; specific, technical terms*
★ Organization of message:	*Primacy*
Nonverbal elements: ★ clothing: ★ gestures: ★ movement:	*Neutral* *A few, small, illustrative gestures.* *Don't move into audience; stay behind podium or move next to podium.*
★ Interest elements: type:	*Stories regarding product, analogies* *Visual aids — charts*
★ Equipment needed:	*Easel for charts*
★ Your primary communication style:	

RATIONALE: The users were technical engineers. Most technical people tend to be Intellects, thus the predominant audience style was Intellect. As technicians, the group was not high powered, therefore neutral attire was most suitable. Intellects use multi-syllabic and specific, technical language. They relate well to those who use similar language patterns. They also prefer to hear their messages delivered in a primacy mode which is their method of

RATIONALE *(continued)*:

organizing messages. After three speakers, any group will begin to fatigue. To maintain interest, a variety as well as quantity of interest elements was needed. Gestures would have added some interest but needed to be small and illustrative to avoid distracting the Intellect style. Intellects prefer distance; this movement should have been limited to the area around the podium. Humor was omitted due to difficulty of selection for an Intellect audience.

Stories were related specifically to the product because Intellects become impatient with personal experiences of the speaker. Analogies could have added another interest dimension without creating a barrier for the Intellect audience.

Charts were selected as the visual aid due to the large size of the audience, and because the third speaker had used slides.

Case Study #2 — Charity Promotion

Audience:	Professionals, community leaders, executives
Size:	200
Location:	Hotel banquet room, set up with dinner tables, 10 people at each table
Time of presentation:	8:00 p.m. After dinner
Topic:	Promotion for a charity
Speaking order:	1st (The only speaker)
Length of presentation:	1 hour

Given the above information, analyze the starred factors, and then give your rationale for your answer at the bottom of the page. Turn to page 168 to check your answer.

★ Style of audience:	
★ Type of language:	
★ Organization of message:	
Nonverbal Elements: ★ clothing: ★ gestures: ★ movement:	
★ Interest elements: type:	
★ Equipment needed:	
★ Your primary communication style:	

RATIONALE:

Summary

Visual aids can be intentionally gimmicky. Flashy visual displays do appeal to certain types of audiences. Visual aids can also serve as a help. By graphically recording important points, your recall of information is aided. Visual aids are an excellent instructional tool and can be used effectively with practice. So, if you were not previously using visual aids because you thought they were too gimmicky, teacherish, or difficult, then consider their advantages. Visual aids are primarily used to:

- reduce distortion
- increase understanding
- increase speed
- increase retention

The types of visual aids that provide these advantages include:

- charts
- graphs
- pictures
- overhead transparencies
- slides
- handouts

In determining your selection of the visual aid to use, consider:

- Purpose of presentation
    entertain: boards, slides, flipcharts
    impress: multi-image slides, boards, handouts
    persuade: boards, slides, overheads, handouts
    inform: flipcharts, chalkboards, overheads, boards or handouts
- Audience type
    Driver: multi-colored visuals
    Evolution or revelation techniques
    Intellect: uncluttered graphs or diagrams
    Amiable: illustrative pictures
    Passive: simplistic charts
- Audience size
    1–50: charts, boards, overheads, slides, flipcharts, chalkboard
    50–100: overheads, slides, boards
    100+ : slides

Once you have selected the visual aid, then practice using it as you practice your speech. Handle any mistakes calmly. Most importantly, be prepared to deliver your message *without* visual accompaniment.

CHAPTER NINE

OF SPECIAL CONSIDERATION

Introducing the Speaker	**Moderating a Meeting**
Questions and Answers	**Reading a Manuscript**

Now that you've mastered audience analysis, the development of your organizational skills, and the integration of interest elements and visual aids within a presentation, you can approach any public speaking situation with a feeling of comfort and control—comfort in understanding the process, and control in knowing how to adapt your communication style to any type of audience. However, before you get too comfortable, it is important to consider certain situations that are often mishandled by experienced as well as novice speakers. The introduction, the role of moderator, question and answer sessions and manuscript reading—each of these topics requires special techniques. Chapter Nine is devoted to a discussion and illustration of these four items of special consideration.

INTRODUCING A SPEAKER

BE: Wonder Word, when I'm asked to introduce a speaker at either a social or business gathering, do I follow the same procedure? Does your matrix apply to every speaking situation? Do I need an opening grabber, thesis, three main points, and a conclusion? I really like that system . . . can I use it in this situation?

Ⓦ   Why are you getting so excited, Bob? You just asked me at least five questions and haven't given me the chance to address one of them yet.

BE: I know, I know. It's just that I remembered that my boss, Mr. Watson, asked me to introduce the guest lecturer at our next marketing meeting. I don't want any more disasters, especially in front of Mr. Watson. What do I do?

Ⓦ   The first thing you do is calm down. Try some deep breathing, Bob. Then let's consider the special circumstances involved in an introduction.

BE: I knew it! Here it is, hours after we started, and I have to begin at the beginning again. This may be the longest day of my life!

Ⓦ   And the most profitable, I might add. Remember when we talked about barriers to listening. How do you typically react during an introduction?

BE: I usually don't hear a thing. That's why I had so many questions for you. When I used to listen to introductions, they all said just about the same thing, so I stopped listening—boredom, I imagine.

Ⓦ I'm not surprised. I haven't heard any good ones myself of late. I want to make sure I answer your questions, Bob, because I may need someone to introduce me sometime. Best it be someone I've tutored.

BE: Good! tell me how can I put some *pazazz* into my introductions.

Ⓦ You don't want too much *pazazz* or you'll steal the show from the main speaker. On the other hand, the speech to introduce should capture audience interest. The purpose of an introduction is to set the stage for the speaker. Read this introduction, Bob, and tell me your reactions.

Our speaker tonight is someone who really needs no introduction. He's been around a number of years and I'm certain he is the best in his field—we are really very fortunate to have him here tonight. So, without further ado, it is with great pleasure that I introduce Dr. John Knowitall, who will be speaking on a topic dear to his heart—"Our rising cost of living."

BE: That's it, Wonder Word! That's the introduction I've heard countless times before. I think it's all the cliches that turn me off. Absolutely no originality or creativity. Also, since you've keyed me into an awareness of language choice, I react negatively to that tentative, non-specific language—"someone," "around," "number of years," "his field"—I really don't know anything about Dr. Knowitall except that he likes the rising cost of living. I can't say that I'm motivated to listen to him, either. Do you have a better example?

Ⓦ Read on, Bob.

"When our president appointed me program chairman for the year, I invited all of you to submit a list of topics you would like addressed at our meetings. The most frequently mentioned was that of how to cope with the rapid rise in the cost of living index. I know you are all as concerned about our shrinking dollar as I am—last year our dinners only cost $10.00—this year the same dinner is costing us $15.00.

How do we cope? To address this issue, I invited Dr. John Knowitall, Professor of Economics at Hale University. In 1978, he was appointed a member of the President's Economic Advisory Board. For the past three years he has been researching ways for all of us to beat the effects of our shrinking dollar.

Dr. Knowitall, we welcome you.''

BE: *This* Dr. Knowitall sounds much more interesting than the other one! I would be interested in hearing this presentation.

Ⓦ What made the difference for you, Bob?

BE: Well, I know more about the speaker—his background, profession, and special recognition. He must know what he's talking about if he was chosen for the President's Economic Advisory Board. If he can advise the President, he's welcome to advise me.

Ⓦ Did any thing else strike you about that introduction?

BE: Most importantly, I felt the speaker was chosen for me, because of my input regarding a list of meeting topics. And it sure "hit home" when he mentioned that our dinners had gone up from $10.00 to $15.00. I had a real reason to listen, plus a personal involvement in the choice.

Ⓦ Very good, Bob. You understood the two main requirements of an introductory speech: it should establish the credibility of the speaker, and secondly, provide the audience with a reason to listen. In short, an introduction must address the questions, *why* this speaker and *why* this topic, for this particular audience. In gathering and organizing biographical data, you include four major points: 1) Who is the speaker? (name, title); 2) Where does the speaker come from? (company, organization; city, state, when appropriate); 3) What are the speaker's qualifications? (education, business track record, publications, honors, awards, affiliations); and 4) Why should the audience listen? (specific importance of topic to audience, and/or speaker's reputation).

BE: As usual, you've made it easy for me, Wonder Word. What do you think of this?

One of my major responsibilities as a marketing representative for Watson, Inc. is to deliver both formal and informal presentations to potential clients. Many of you have indicated that the ability to organize your ideas and present them in a creative, persuasive fashion is of utmost concern to you.

This morning I have invited Wonder Word, an authority on presentations, to address this interest and need. Wonder Word has developed specific strategies to assist you in the design and preparation of your marketing presentations. Although he has worked with thousands of public speakers, Wonder Word takes a personal interest in individual styles, so that your final presentation will reflect *you*. Please welcome Wonder Word.''

Ⓦ I am impressed. I just may ask you to introduce me at my next conference. Let me suggest several techniques to employ when delivering an introductory speech:

- Practice it—do *not* read
- Verify your introduction with the speaker prior to delivery—check pronunciation and pertinent data
- Pause until audience is quiet
- Use your normal voice and speaking style
- Direct all comments to the audience
- View yourself as a scene setter—not the show
- Move away from the lectern, but remain standing until the speaker is in place.
- Listen like you have never been so entertained before—be a model listener.

BE: Okay, Wonder Word, I wrote those points down. But another area of concern for me is when I have to not only introduce the speaker(s), but also serve as a moderator for a meeting, panel discussion, conference workshop, etc.—all those situations where the responsibility for flow and continuity lie with the facilitator. You haven't failed me yet. Can you turn me into a model moderator?

Ⓦ If you had asked me that yesterday, I would have thought ''no,'' but you've made such progress during these few hours, I'm inclined to think I can perform that miracle too. The moderator of a meeting—i.e., group discussion—has two sets of objectives and responsibilities. Prior to the discussion, the moderator assumes responsibility for planning the meeting. The plan should include an agenda to structure the discussion, interest elements to stimulate and maintain attention, and questions to generate participation.

BE: The *before* is the easy part. It's at the meeting itself that problems happen. Either the agenda is inappropriate, or the group doesn't participate, or someone dominates the discussion, leading it off track. I've been to enough meetings to have witnessed these developments time after time. You've got to be made of steel to put up with all that.

Ⓦ I never said it would be easy, Bob. But if the moderator is sensitive to the group (its needs and responses), and is aware of his responsibilities, he can create an excellent atmosphere where active participation can achieve the desired results. During the meeting, the moderator has many responsibilities. The first is to clearly state the objectives of the discussion. When appropriate, canvass the audience for their objectives and expectations. Another major task is to provide a time frame. As official clockwatcher, it is important to start on time, end on time, and call any break as necessary. If at the end of the appointed time, participants would like to continue the discussion, dismiss those who wish to leave, and invite interested members to stay.

BE: I really admire someone who can stay on schedule.

Ⓦ I agree, Bob—although there are times when a pre–established agenda needs to be adjusted. It is the moderator's responsibility to reassess the proposed agenda to determine whether need and/or interest will change the established format. The moderator can choose to rely solely on his or her own personal judgment or request group consensus. The attitude, enthusiasm, and direction of the moderator are crucial to establishing a climate for group participation. When discussion slows, the moderator can stimulate through questioning and soliciting other opinions. The moderator is also responsible for answering questions, or redirecting them to other group members for response. And, finally, it is essential for the moderator to maintain control of the discussion, to keep it on track, yet to provide an opportunity for expressing different viewpoints.

BE: Quite a job. I don't think I'll sign up for moderator just yet. Your description makes delivering a presentation sound enjoyable by comparison.

(W) It *is* a demanding role because of the balance between group participation and control. Here again, the opening is vital in establishing interest and setting the tone as well as the expectations for the session.

Since I'm such an authority, I usually am involved in solo presentations, but there was a time when I acted as group moderator. These introductory guidelines always served me well:

1. Welcome the group. Establish rapport, list personal qualifications.
2. If there is a guest presenter, introduce him or her (see ''The speech to introduce.'')
3. State the topic and explain why it was selected.
4. Ask the participants open questions about their expectations for the session.
5. If the audience is small (25 or fewer), ask each person to introduce self, company and expectations.
6. State the objectives of the session (in light of audience expectations and personal goals); outline what is to be accomplished.
7. Explain how the session and the achievement of the objectives will benefit the participants.
8. Provide a brief overview of the session—an organization of points and time frame.
9. Advise the audience when you will invite questions (specifically when panel or guest speaker are used).
10. Display interest and enthusiasm.

BE: That's a good list, Wonder Word. But I was at a conference in Cincinnati last year and, after the panel members had presented their information, chaos ensued. There was one fellow who kept interrupting, everyone was talking at once, and another person erroneously interpreted statistical evidence. The moderator was helpless!

(W) I worked with someone in Cincinnati recently . . . he was very interested in improving his skills as a moderator. Hmmm . . . well, at any rate, I showed him the following grid. It identifies typical participant responses, why they happen, and what you can do about it.

Participant response	Why it happens	What you can do
Rambling	natural style	ask specific questions
	recency communicator	when he/she takes a breath, cut in, thank the speaker, clarify point, and go on.
	Amiable; likes spot-light	move in
		paraphrase ideas
Side Conversation	reaction to subject	move in (don't embarrass)
	personal comments	pause, take break
	antagonist vs. leader/moderator	ask one to repeat
		compliment—their viewpoints are important
		contract to discuss date (in session or private)
Erroneous Comment	incorrect information misinterpretation	clarify through questions
		empathize with feelings
		restate or summarize correct information
Interruption	primacy communicator	move away
	reacts to others' styles	redirect discussion to another issue or other participant
	rude	ask him/her to summarize issue before pro-ceeding to different topic
	well informed and has answers	review agenda for items to be discussed in session
Hostile Reaction	prior negative experience	compliment, assign important function
	unsolved problems	primacy—admit problem justified, en route to solution
	feels neglected, left out, ignored	probe to clarify their view, opinion—use Amiable/Intellect style
	impatient	

BE: I like the way you organize your information, Wonder Word, but your technical jargon has confused me again. What do you mean by "paraphrase," "contract," "probe"?

Ⓦ You're right, Bob. I tell you to adapt, and sometimes even *I* forget. There are certain techniques for dealing with problem participants. The goal is to assist them in regaining an adult style of communication—logical, reasonable, and factual. The techniques include: 1) paraphrasing—restating an idea or opinion for accuracy of message heard; 2) providing alternatives—allowing two or three choices of action; 3) probing—questioning for further information or to clarify; 4) providing feedback—finding something positive to say before stating problem or concern; and 5) contracting—designating specific shared responsibilities for both parties.

BE: I've never called those techniques by name, but I have used some of those steps in dealing with my staff at the office. Although I understand that process, I find it difficult to implement all the time.

Ⓦ Bob, I am acutely aware of the significant differences between you and me. Suffice it to say that I would not be sharing this information with you if it were not in the realm of possibility that you could incorporate and use these techniques. But, an example might help. When I was in Cincinnati, one participant in the group became upset over the increased year—end sales quota. He felt that changing the quota mid—year was unfair.

BE: I don't blame him. I'd be upset myself.

Ⓦ But that's not the point of this discussion. The point is to show you how the adult processing techniques work, remember? Since you feel so strongly about the above topic, perhaps we could play act a scene or, as people call it in training circles, a role play. You pretend that I'm the moderator of the meeting and attack me concerning the unfair nature of the new policy.

BE: This is the first time anyone ever gave me permission to get mad at them. Let's start. Are you ready?

Ⓦ Anytime you are!

Suddenly Bob leaps up and starts yelling at Wonder Word. One hand rests on his hip, the other he uses to shake his finger at the imaginary executives.

BE: Just who do those sales managers think they are! They never think about the people out in the field. They *never* take reality into consideration. They just pull those quotas out of a hat!

Paraphrase

Ⓦ As I understand it, you think that the corporate office doesn't take into consideration the real potential in your territories, and you think they are being unrealistic in their quotas,—is that right?

BE: Well, yes.

Feedback

Ⓦ I see. You know, Bob, I can understand why you would be frustrated. I would be, too, if someone were not using a fair criterion to judge my performance. The corporate managers do appreciate your viewpoint of the situation. After all, you know your territory better than anyone else.

BE: You've got it right there.

Probing

Ⓦ What do you think would be a better way for the corporation to use your knowledge?

BE: Well, I don't know. I haven't thought about that.

Contracting

Ⓦ Why don't we see if anyone else in the group has any ideas and, if you think of anything, bring up your thought for discussion. Is that all right with you?

BE: Sure. You're truly amazing. Even though I knew what you were doing, you *still* calmed me down. The interesting thing is, you didn't answer the question regarding the new quota.

Ⓦ Sometimes you don't have to come up with the answers, Bob. Many times people get upset because they feel no one will listen to their viewpoint. When you show your concern and interest as you use the adult processing, the need for anger is removed. From that point, you can discuss the issues logically.

BE: You really know your material, Wonder Word, but I'll never be able to stay calm and use your techniques too.

Ⓦ Did you learn to ride a bike in one day? Skills need exercise to develop. I suggest that you begin exercising some new muscles. I'm still concerned, and so should you be, with the possibility of question and answer sessions. Your audience was so bored and tired this time that they didn't ask you any questions. How would you handle difficult questions? Mind you, I don't advocate putting your audience to sleep to avoid questions.

When responding to questions, it is vital for you to maintain control, both verbally and non-verbally. Visual control can be maintained through adopting a comfortable posture which creates a positive image. Another nonverbal response is to disengage eye contact after the question is raised. You can redirect information to the entire group, thereby detracting attention from the questioner. In addition, the speaker can turn or move away from the questioner to reestablish rapport with the group.

BE: I never would have thought of that.

Ⓦ It's also essential to maintain verbal control during the question and answer period. View each question as a continued forum for your position. Use primacy organization to respond to all positive aspects, and recency in reaction to negative aspects. If a question is difficult, rephrase it to your advantage. For example, "Mr. President, why can't you do anything to stop inflation?" can be rephrased by the President as "You are concerned about the shrinking value of the dollar." If someone poses a two or more-part question, respond in the order to enhance your position, or only answer one part. Skilled speakers have learned how to relabel emotional terms, so that the Three-Mile Island *disaster* became an *incident*. If the topic is extremely emotional, empathize with the feelings of the audience (I can understand why you are so upset.) If you don't know an answer, either 1) redirect the question to another source, 2) redirect the question to the audience, or 3) indicate that the information is currently unavailable, and 4) state your follow-up plan for obtaining that information. An important underlying theme in handling questions is to be *brief*. Often the more you try to explain, the more ensnarled you become, so avoid the temptation to cover every angle of a question.

BE: When I get my second chance to present the new Watson machines, I can expect some difficult questions. I'll really need to practice my nervousness techniques then.

Ⓦ Bob, the best response is *preparation*. Always anticipate potential questions and objections before your presentation. I'm sure you have a good idea of likely questions. Using the organizational matrix as a basis, think of five questions or objections to your presentation and how you would respond.

Bob's Questions and Answers

Question/Objection	*My Responses*
1. Will the service be any better than what we're getting now?	The service will match and surpass the fine response we've always given our customers. We've hired a staff of ten technicians especially for these machines and we'll be adding more as our entrance into the marketplace increases.
2. Do you have the current stock to meet our demands?	We have fifty systems ready to go. As demands increase, our delivery format will limit delays to a maximum of ten weeks.
3. Do you *really* have all the bugs worked out? When your original machines first came out on the market, it took you two years to get all the kinks fixed.	I appreciate your concern. Watson, Inc. was acutely aware of the need to design a trouble-free system. That's why we delayed entering the marketplace. The new machines have been field tested for the past two years. We are confident that our systems are ready for you.

Question/Objection	*My Responses*
4. We're a small operation. If we don't change to the computerized machines, will our service suffer?	Not at all, we've hired a staff of ten technicians especially for the new line. Your service will not be affected in any way.
5. Will your machines be more expensive than the one that ACME came out with recently?	Our line is a more sophisticated system which includes a variety of different features to improve your productivity. Our machines, though priced somewhat higher than ACME's, will be well worth the extra money you invest.

Now it's your turn. Based on the presentation you have developed, plan five objections/questions and your responses.

Questions/Objections	*My Responses*
1.	
2.	
3.	
4.	
5.	

READING A MANUSCRIPT

The one item that remains to be discussed with special consideration is the rare occasion when you must *read* a speech. Although the naturally-spoken, conversational presentation is recommended, there are instances when reading is necessary—either because of the length of the speech, or the unfamiliar technical nature of the information. The goal, even when reading, is to make the speech sound conversational, yet professional.

To achieve this goal it is necessary to score the manuscript and practice the scored piece. The first step is to score the phrasing. As you read the speech out loud, make slash marks at natural pauses, creating a phrasing pattern. Retype the speech with one phrase per line, triple spaced. This method reduces the risk of losing your place while providing adequate space for scoring rate and gestures. As you read the speech aloud, where rate quickens, draw an arrow; where it decreases, draw three dots. To score gestures, identify the important phrases or words; select appropriate gestures which reinforce the meaning of the verbal message; then mark the manuscript for gestures. Finally, to ensure a natural tone, tape record your reading of the scored manuscript and review for accuracy of phrasing and intonation.

Manuscript Symbols

/   Pause

⟶   Speed up

...   Slow down

↝   Gesture

Summary

Although most presentations follow the organizational matrix, there are special circumstances which require additional planning and application of new techniques.

When introducing a speaker, the most important concerns are

1. establishing speaker credibility, and
2. providing the audience with a reason for listening.

Moderator responsibilities require prior planning as well as control throughout the session. Control extends to the proposed agenda, the time frame, the discussion flow, and the participant response. Techniques for controlling difficult participants include paraphrasing, probing, providing alternatives, providing positive feedback, and contracting.

In question and answer sessions, both visual and verbal control are important. Verbally, the speaker can use the question period as a continued forum for his or her own viewpoint. Nonverbally, the speaker can break eye contact or move away from a hostile questioner.

If a speech must be read, the goal is to produce a conversational tone. Scoring for phrases, rate and gestures in addition to recorded practice sessions will enhance the natural quality of a read speech.

CHAPTER TEN

READY, SET, GO!

BE: Wonder Word, I have to hand it to you! You have covered *every* aspect of effective presentations. Initially, I just wanted to learn how to organize my ideas, control nervousness, and be more interesting. But you've given me *everything*—how to help my audience listen, how to understand and adapt communication styles, how to use gestures, visual aids and other interest elements, how to introduce a speaker, handle questions, read a manuscript . . . I can't wait to put all of this information to use.

Ⓦ Bob, I've given you a lot of information and I know that mentally you have absorbed it all, but you're still missing an important step. *Practice!* You've got to integrate gestures, walking patterns and visual aids into your presentation.

BE: Wonder Word, when am I going to get my second chance? You're always coming up with another step and another step and another step . . .

Ⓦ Keep climbing, Bob, you're almost there. First get ready by practicing. Then learn how to read your audience. By reading your audience, you can evaluate your presentation for effectiveness as you go along, and adapt when necessary. Then you'll be ready to start.

Bob, like most of us, is anxious to apply all of the techniques and information in a "real" situation. Wonder Word, however, is right. First you need to practice. The amount of time spent practicing will differ from person to person. The objective is to practice until your speech flows smoothly. To create a smoothly flowing speech, select the language you will use, integrate gestures, determine your walking pattern, and practice with and without visual aids.

Practicing will provide you with an opportunity to transform your thoughts into words. Through repetition your language patterns are reinforced so that you sound natural and conversational. Repetition will also help to eliminate groping for words once you stand before your audience. As you make statements or pose questions, determine the gestures you will use to underscore your verbal message.

If you plan to walk into the audience, or move to the side of the podium, determine the point in your speech when you should begin moving so that you are not in transit when starting an important point. Also, plan your movement when you need to refer to a visual aid.

Wonder Word takes Bob through these last steps.

(W) Bob, say the phrase in your speech where you talk about meeting the demand for computerized production. Don't *read* the section.

BE: O.K., Wonder Word. In my speech I say,

There is an increasing need for computerized production today and we are meeting this need so that,—I mean with the most sophisticated technology available.

What I meant to say is . . .

There is an increasing demand for computerized devices today, and we are meeting this demand with a computerized machine that reflects our sophisticated age of technology.

Now I understand what you mean about language. Practice so I can say what I mean to say.

(W) Right. What do you say next?

BE: Next, I list the ways that our product meets the demand.

(W) What gesture could you use for listing?

BE: Well, just before I give my list I can walk to the side of the podium, and as I list each point I could slice the air with my hand.

(W) Good; only don't slice the air, just raise your right arm up with the palm of your hand facing down and your fingers closed. Then make a small downward movement as you say each point. Now, when do you want to use your boards?

BE: I use one board next as I talk about the dimensions.

(W) Practice walking over to your board, remove the blank board on top of the one you want to display, then point to each item. Remember, as you speak, face your audience and maintain eye contact. When you finish, practice your speech without your boards just as a precautionary measure.

Just as Bob has done, practice your speech to reinforce language, gestures, walking patterns and use of visual aids. Also, practice without visual accompaniment.

As you go through your practice sessions, time your speech. Make sure that you do not go too far under or too far over the allotted time.

Request that a friend, spouse, or associate keep track of the time and act as your audience. Practicing before an audience will provide you with live feedback and allow you to make any necessary changes before the final presentation. Chances are, if you are extremely nervous, have difficulty expressing your thoughts, or move awkwardly before your "practice" audience, you will also present the same image to your final audience. As a substitute for a practice audience, you could videotape your practice sessions. Many companies now have training facilities with videotape equipment. Investigate to determine whether or not such equipment is available to you.

At this point, your speech flows smoothly and you are prepared to face your audience. Well, almost. The last phase of your preparation stage involves preparing for unforeseen obstacles or barriers. How would you be affected if the speaker before you gave an hour speech instead of a half-hour speech, and the audience fatigued more quickly than you had anticipated? How would you react if someone in your audience began whispering or came in late and disrupted other audience members? These potential barriers could have a negative impact unless you are able to read your audience's feedback and adapt your presentation accordingly.

As mentioned in Chapter Two, feedback can be verbal or nonverbal. During a presentation, the type of feedback you receive will primarily be on a nonverbal level. When reading nonverbal feedback, consider your audience as a whole while observing individual responses. There are four main areas for reading nonverbal signals: facial and head movements, hand and arm movements, trunk positions, and leg and foot movements. If the people in your audience are smiling and shaking their heads up and down, then these signals can be interpreted as positive, and changes in your presentation are not necessary. Frowns or yawns, however, are negative signals suggesting that your audience is disagreeing or disinterested. Be aware, though, that facial expressions can be easily contrived and controlled. A person's leg and foot movements, however, are the most difficult and least likely to be controlled. Leg and foot movements, therefore, are better indicators of a person's level of interest. For a general overview of these four areas and what the various movements indicate, review the grid on the following page. Our friend Bob still doesn't understand the significance of reading your audience.

Nonverbal Feedback Grid

TYPES	POSITIVE	NEUTRAL	NEGATIVE
Facial and Head Movements	smile shaking "yes" no movement	head tilted no identifiable expression	frown shaking "no" asleep
Hand and Arm Movements	no movement clapping taking notes	slight movement taking notes	folded arms much movement doodling
Trunk Positions	leaning forward	vertical	slumped back or forward
Leg and Foot Movements	fast bouncing of foot or feet no movement	slight shifts	slow bouncing of foot or feet shifting of legs

BE: Wonder Word, I thought you were going to make me dynamic, but now you've got me worrying about what everybody else is doing. Whether they're interested or not depends on me, doesn't it?

Ⓦ Yes, Bob, their level of interest does depend on you, but you will maintain their interest only if you're prepared for the unknown. If barriers occur that detract from your presentation or if your audience becomes unresponsive to your message for any reason, then it is up to you to regain their attention. Use the information on the grid as a barometer for gauging interest; then adapt.

BE: I can't make adjustments. I've already practiced and refined my speech.

Ⓦ I'm not suggesting that you alter your entire speech, but learn to be a bit flexible. If you find that someone has become unattentive, direct a question to them regarding a point you've recently made. However, if the person does not know the answer, don't dwell so the person becomes embarrassed, just move on to someone you know has been listening.

BE: I know they'll listen after that. What are some more ideas?

Ⓦ Move into the audience and stand next to the person who is unattentive. This always gets their attention even though you are not speaking to them directly.

BE: What about eye contact? Couldn't you just stand by the podium and stare at them?

Ⓦ Your objective is not to stare them down, Bob. Just engage and maintain eye contact for a few seconds. Eye contact is another excellent technique for regaining attention. Maybe you should give this lecture instead of me.

BE: Well I don't know about you, Wonder Word, but when I lost my audience, I wanted to pack up and leave.

Ⓦ Sometimes, Bob, that is exactly what you should do. If you've tried the other techniques and still fail to capture their interest, then summarize your speech and conclude early.

BE: I like that idea, Wonder Word, but I didn't think stopping early would ever be appropriate. What I did was rush through my presentation.

Ⓦ The problem with rushing as you did is that you were no longer in control of yourself or your presentation. Deliberately changing the pace of your delivery can, however, be effective in renewing interest if you remain in control. In addition to accelerating your rate, you may also try changing your volume. Speak louder or softer for contrast. Adapting during your talk is the last step in delivering an effective presentation. This will ensure that the communication process remains intact.

BE: How will I know if I'm successful? How can I judge my performance?

Ⓦ First, get your analysis form ready. I won't be back to tell you how you did, so you've got to evaluate your own performance.

BE: Wonder Word, can't you stay to listen? You've worked so hard to make me a success.

Ⓦ No, Bob, *you've* worked hard to make *you* a success and I can't stay to evaluate your performance. Duty calls. I must attend to that lady in L.A. The only way you will continue to improve is to analyze your presentation and review each technique we've discussed.

BE: Okay, Wonder Word, show me the evaluation form. I'll mail it to you when it's over.

Ⓦ Don't worry, Bob, I'll know how you did; I wouldn't miss it for anything.

Following is the evaluation form and directions Bob will use.

Evaluation Sheet

As soon as possible following your presentation, fill out this evaluation sheet. Look at each of the elements and record the style you incorporated, the gestures used, their impact on your audience, and future recommendations for change.

VISUAL

Elements for Review	Style(s) Incorporated	Describe Those You Used	Impact on Audience	Recommendations for Future
Gestures				
Standing Postures				
Seated Postures				
Walking				
Facial Expressions				

VERBAL

Elements for Review	Style(s) Incorporated	Describe Those You Used	Impact on Audience	Recommendations for Future
Language Choice				
Vocal Quality				
Rate of Delivery				
Volume				
Verbal Pauses				

1. Did you complete an audience analysis?
2. Did you correctly identify the style of your audience?
3. What was your audience's primary style?
4. Were you able to maintain your audience's interest?
5. If members of your audience lost interest, what techniques did you employ to regain their attention?

Ⓦ One last assignment, Bob—you still need to fill out the last item on your case study.

BE: That's right, Wonder Word. I still need to fill in my primary communication style for the presentation.

Ⓦ So, what do you think?

BE: Looking at the list of factors makes it easy. I'd have Intellect as my primary style.

Ⓦ That's why I put that last, Bob. Analyzing all of the elements you use to present to different audiences tells you what your primary style will be.

You need to complete your case study along with Bob. Following case study #2 there are case studies #3 and #4. Fill out both to make sure you fully understand all of the factors necessary to adapt your style to different audiences. The answers for all of the case studies begin on page 168.

Bob's Case Study

Audience:	Users of product, usually technical engineers
Size:	100
Location:	Large room: seating capacity 300, set-up theatre style
Time of presentation:	4:00 (last speech of the day)
Topic:	Introduction of new product
Speaking order:	4th
Length of presentation:	½ hour

Given the above information, analyze the starred factors. Wonder Word's answer is at the bottom of the page.

★Style of audience:	Intellect
★Type of language:	Multi-syllabic words; specific, technical terms
★Organization of message:	Primacy
Nonverbal elements: ★ clothing: ★ gestures: ★ movement:	Neutral A few, small, illustrative gestures. Don't move into audience; stay behind podium or move next to podium.
★Interest elements: type:	Stories regarding product, analogies Visual aids — charts
★Equipment needed:	Easel for charts
★Your primary communication style:	Intellect

RATIONALE: The users were technical engineers. Most technical people tend to be Intellects, thus the predominant audience style was Intellect. As technicians, the group was not high powered; therefore, neutral attire was most suitable. Intellects use multi-syllabic and specific, technical language. They relate well to those who use similar language patterns.

RATIONALE *(continued)*:
They also prefer to hear their messages delivered in a primacy mode, which is their method of organizing messages.

After three speakers, any group will begin to fatigue. To maintain interest, a variety as well as quantity of interest elements are needed. Gestures will add some interest but must be small and illustrative to avoid distracting the Intellect style. Intellects prefer distance; this movement should be limited to the area around the podium. Humor was omitted due to difficulty of selection for an Intellect audience. Stories should relate specifically to the product because Intellects become impatient with personal experiences of the speaker. Analogies will add another interest dimension without creating a barrier for the Intellect audience.

Charts were selected as the visual aid due to the large size of the audience, and because the third speaker had used slides.

The different elements listed would create an Intellect communication style for the presenter.

Case Study #2 — Charity Promotion

Audience:	Professionals, community leaders, executives
Size:	200
Location:	Hotel banquet room, set up with dinner tables, 10 people at each table
Time of presentation:	8:00 p.m. After dinner
Topic:	Promotion for a charity
Speaking order:	1st (The only speaker)
Length of presentation:	1 hour

Given the above information, analyze the starred factors, and then give your rationale for your answer at the bottom of the page. Turn to page 168 to check your answer.

★Style of audience:	
★Type of language:	
★Organization of message:	
Nonverbal elements: ★ clothing: ★ gestures: ★ movement:	
★Interest elements: type:	
★Equipment needed:	
★Your primary communication style:	

RATIONALE:

Case Study #3 — Rotary Club Meeting

Audience:	Rotary Club members
Size:	50
Location:	Public hall. Seating capacity 100, set up theatre style
Time of presentation:	1:00 p.m. (after lunch)
Topic:	Report on club sponsored activity
Speaking order:	1st
Length of presentation:	40 minutes, including question & answer session

Given the above information, analyze the following factors to maximize effectiveness with this audience.

Style of audience:	
Type of language:	
Organization of message:	

Nonverbal elements:
    clothing:
    gestures:
    movement:	

Interest elements: type:	
Equipment needed:	
Your primary communication style:	

RATIONALE:

Case Study #4 — Meeting of Company Secretaries

Audience:	Secretaries
Size:	25
Location:	Company cafeteria, set up 4–5 per table
Time of presentation:	6:00 p.m. (After dinner)
Topic:	Company policy
Speaking order:	2nd
Length of presentation:	½ hour

Given the above information, analyze the following factors to maximize effectiveness with this audience.

Style of audience:	
Type of language:	
Organization of message:	
Nonverbal elements: clothing: gestures: movement:	
Interest elements: type:	
Equipment needed:	
Your primary communication style:	

RATIONALE:

Bob is also referred again to Chapter 1 to evaluate whether or not he met his objectives in the areas he felt needed improvement.

As Bob has done, complete these analysis forms following your next presentation. Update the information each time you speak. Only through continued monitoring and review can you expect to continually improve. If you find that being objective about your own performance is difficult, seek assistance from a professional in the area of public speaking. Our professional, Wonder Word, has guided and directed you, but the task of utilizing this information is up to *you*. To further assist you in your review of this book, periodically answer the questionnaire on pages 164–165.

Summary

Bob is anxious to put everything that he has learned to use. Wonder Word, however, reminds him that he is not yet ready. There are two more preparation stages: (1) practice, then (2) learn techniques that will regain the attention of an audience in the event of unforeseen barriers.

- Practice until your speech flows naturally
    Reinforce language patterns
    Integrate gestures
    Determine walking patterns
    Practice with visual aids
    Practice without visual aids

The amount of time spent in practice depends on your individual needs. It is advantageous to practice with an audience or on videotape. Your audience can time your speech as well as provide feedback on your performance.

The second stage entails reading audience feedback during the actual presentation. Most of the feedback received will be on a nonverbal level. To read nonverbal feedback, observe the movement and expressions of selected individuals. There are four areas of the body to consider:

- Facial and head movements
- Hand and arm movements
- Trunk positions
- Leg and foot movements

Each of these areas send signals which can then be interpreted as positive, neutral, or negative. When you begin to receive negative signals which indicate a lack of interest, employ the following techniques:

- Direct a question to an audience member
- Move into the audience
- Establish eye contact
- Change pace of delivery; change rate, or volume
- Summarize and conclude presentation

You're now ready to present your information and control your performance. Continued evaluation and review is the final step. Analyze each performance with the purpose of meeting your objectives to overcome stumbling blocks to public speaking. You have the tools you need to develop and deliver a winning presentation. Wonder Word has done his part; the rest is up to you. Practice, perform, evaluate, and your future presentations will be, Winning Words.

Quiz For Review

To keep you on your toes, periodically take this quiz. Answer each of the following questions by placing a check (√) in the correct box.

	TRUE	FALSE
1. The number of people in your audience will not influence your presentation.		
2. The term recency means that the main point is given first, followed by supportive information.		
3. Nervousness should be controlled but not completely eliminated.		
4. Audiences today are primarily "watchers" rather than "listeners," so your nonverbal communication is extremely important.		
5. It is possible to analyze your primary and secondary style of communication, but because audiences are composed of many different people, a communication style analysis is not appropriate for audiences.		
6. When preparing to read a manuscript, first go through and mark all of your pauses.		
7. A person who uses the Amiable style of communication speaks in generalities, uses the recency format, and uses frequent gestures.		
8. Flipcharts can be used effectively with an audience of 100.		
9. If you have prepared your speech with visual aids, and the visual aids are damaged en route to your presentation, you should postpone or cancel your speaking engagement.		
10. During your presentation, you should use only one interest element per main point.		
11. An Intellect does not need to adapt his style of communication when addressing an Intellect audience.		
12. If during your presentation your audience "shuts down," summarize and conclude your speech.		
13. You should always wear high authority clothes when addressing professional audiences.		

	TRUE	FALSE

14. If you are introducing a speaker, it is not necessary for you to give any information about yourself.

15. Walking into a Passive audience acts as a positive interest element.

16. When you don't have an answer during the question/answer session, it is best to only say "I don't know."

17. In the organizational matrix, the thesis is followed by a statement of your perspective on the topic, and then an introduction of your main points.

18. If you have experience in giving presentations and you've given this information before, there is no need to practice.

19. The sound of your voice and verbal pauses are two examples of paralinguistics.

20. When you give a presentation, you should view it as a conversation with your audience.

Epilogue

BE: I can't believe how much I've learned in just one night. My only concern is that I won't remember it all when I get my second chance.

Ⓦ You have learned a significant amount, Bob, but, you're bright, and I have faith that you'll do well.

BE: But what if I panic, lose my place, lose my nerve—you won't be here to freeze things like you did when we first met. Maybe you should stick around after all.

Ⓦ You won't panic, Bob, you're ready.

BE: I am? Wait a minute, I still need to practice; you said practice is the most important part.

Ⓦ I did say practice is important, but we've done that, remember?

BE: Oh, right. But what about my visual aids—we need to go to my office to get them made.

Ⓦ Look behind you. They are on your easel.

BE: What easel? (An easel stands a few feet from the lectern Bob had used in his presentation. Resting on the lip are the charts Wonder Word had described earlier. Bob swallows hard and turns back to face Wonder Word.) They're done?

Ⓦ Exactly as we discussed.

BE: Wait, Wonder Word, don't leave me yet—I think I need to discuss this with you a little more.

Ⓦ Your second chance is here, Bob. Don't worry, you will succeed. My track record is one of *success*—never a failure. Goodbye, Bob—and good luck!

BE: No, not yet. I can't handle this. I think I'm going to be sick, Wonder Word—*please*!

But it's too late . . . Wonder Word is gone. Stunned by Wonder Word's abrupt departure, Bob remains frozen, eyes searching, arm

outstretched. The reality of Wonder Word's abandonment settles in his mind. He blinks once, twice, then focuses on the microphone he has unknowingly adjusted in his shocked state. The sound of soft applause enters his consciousness and grows louder. He looks beyond the mike and realizes he is standing behind the podium. Before him sits the audience he had addressed earlier. He takes a deep breath and looks down quickly. The air rushes out in relief. The matrix he had pared down so carefully is sitting right where it belongs. A quick glance to the right assures him that his charts are still in place. He looks back to the crowd and notices a man looking up with an encouraging smile. Concentrating on the man's friendly eyes, Bob begins. He lifts his hand to gesture and says, ''How many of you here today, have used motorized machines for over five years? Ten years? Twenty years? How many have hoped that those machines would one day be computerized?'' As Bob continues to speak, members of the audience lean forward with interest. There are still sounds, but now it is the shuffle of paper and the scratching of pens as a few individuals jot down notes. The time comes to refer to the charts. Bob slips the microphone out of the stand, turns and walks towards the easel. The rest of the presentation continues without a hitch. Bob is surprised at how quickly the time rushes by. The half hour is almost gone as he concludes with his ending grabber.
''Ladies and gentlemen, the computer age is here and Watson, Inc. is keeping in step with the times. Those of you that have used our machines with confidence for five, ten, or twenty years, can use our new machines with the same degree of confidence for the next five, ten, or twenty years. Computerized production—a part of the future available to you today.'' The applause echoes through the conference room. Thanks to Wonder Word, Bob's ''second chance'' has been a success.

Case Study #2—Charity Promotion

Audience:	Professionals, community leaders, executives
Size:	200
Location:	Hotel banquet room, set up with dinner tables, 10 people at each table
Time of presentation:	8:00 p.m. (After dinner)
Topic:	Promotion for charity
Speaking order:	1st (The only speaker)
Length of presentation:	1 hour

Style of audience:	Driver
Type of language:	Buzzwords, multi-syllables
Organization of message:	Primacy

Nonverbal elements:
  clothing:
  gestures:
  movement:
	High authority
	Illustrative
	Walk into audience

Interest elements: type:	Humor, stories, vocal quality Quotes, movement
Equipment needed:	Microphone with extension cord
Your primary communication style:	Driver/Amiable

RATIONALE: The audience is composed of highly motivated people in power positions. Their dominant style would be Driver. To adapt, the message should be delivered in a Driver style: energetic, rapid rate of speech, use of buzzwords & polysyllabic words and large gestures. Incorporation of the Amiable style assists in establishing rapport. Along with use of an organizational matrix, a bit of the Intellect style will aid in presenting an organized message. Communicating in the primacy mode is the end objective.

RATIONALE *(continued)*:
Due to this type of speech and large size of audience, visual aids such as charts, slides and overheads are not recommended. This audience would be receptive to humor, quotes and stories. Varied vocal inflection is essential as an interest element. Walking into and interacting with the audience using large, open gestures adds flavor to the presentation.

High authority attire would be representative of this professional group; i.e. navy or pin-striped suit.

Check microphone and physical setup prior to presentation.

Case Study #3 — Rotary Club Meeting

Audience:	Rotary Club members
Size:	50
Location:	Public hall. Seating capacity 100, set up theatre style
Time of presentation:	1:00 p.m. (After lunch)
Topic:	Report on club-sponsored activity
Speaking order:	1st
Length of presentation:	40 minutes, including question & answer session

Style of audience:	Amiable
Type of language:	Personal pronouns, general to specific
Organization of message:	Recency→primacy

Nonverbal elements:
    clothing:
    gestures:
    movement:
	
	Neutral
	Open
	Move into audience

Interest elements: type:	 Flip charts, humor, stories, vocal quality
Equipment needed:	Chart stand Microphone (optional)
Your primary communication style:	Amiable/Intellect

RATIONALE: Amiables like affiliation. An audience of club members would be predominately Amiable. To establish and maintain rapport, adapt the Amiable style of communication by using personal pronouns and general, one–syllable words. To present an organized message, incorporate traits of the Intellect by becoming specific and using the primacy mode. To further assist with organization—important points can be displayed on a flip chart.

RATIONALE *(continued)*:

As interest elements, Amiables are receptive to stories and humor. An expressive vocal quality and movement with open gestures are key in maintaining their attention. Also, it is right after lunch and a time when people feel relaxed, so interest elements are essential.

Depending on your ability to project your voice, a microphone is optional. Check flip chart stand for stability, and make sure the microphone works. Don't forget a marking pen if one is needed.

Neutral attire corresponds with this type of audience, i.e. sports jacket and slacks or dress with a jacket.

Case Study #4 — Meeting of Company Secretaries

Audience:	Secretaries
Size:	25
Location:	Company cafeteria, set up 4–5 per table
Time of presentation:	6:00 p.m.
Topic:	Company policy
Speaking order:	2nd
Length of presentation:	½ hour

Style of audience:	Passive (Primary) Amiable (Secondary)
Type of language:	General→Specific
Organization of message:	Recency→Primacy

Nonverbal elements:
   clothing:
   gestures:
   movement:
	
	Neutral
	Limited
	Limited

Interest elements: type:	Vocal quality, flip chart, humor
Equipment needed:	Flip chart stand
Your primary communication style:	Amiable/Intellect

RATIONALE: If you are imparting company policy, your position will more than likely be on a higher level than that of the group being addressed. As an authority figure addressing non-decision makers, the general audience style will be Passive. If you were to communicate to them as a Driver, your audience would be overwhelmed and barriers created. Communicating as a Passive would make you appear too tentative and unsure of yourself. A mixture of Amiable and Intellect is most appropriate. Characteristics of the Amiable style would in-

RATIONALE *(continued)*:

clude use of personal pronouns and a story to create rapport. Language and organization would move from the general to the specific, thereby putting you into an Intellect mode.

Nonverbally, reflect the style of the group. Display few gestures, remain primarily stationary, and dress in neutral attire.

To appear Amiable as well as maintain interest, use vocal inflection, a story as the grabber, and a flip chart to illustrate points.

Since the setting is the cafeteria, arrange 4 or 5 people to a table. A microphone is not needed for this size group; however, bring a chart stand for the flip chart.

Review Quiz Answer Sheet

	TRUE	FALSE
1. The size of the audience influences your selection of visual aids and whether or not equipment such as a microphone is needed.		X
2. Recency means that supportive information is given prior to the main point. Primacy means the main point is given first followed by supportive information.		X
3. Nervousness should be controlled and channeled to create positive energy.	X	
4. According to research, up to 87% of our messages are interpreted on a nonverbal level.	X	
5. Audiences, as a whole, tend to take on a primary style. For example, people in technical fields tend to be Intellects in style.		X
6. Read the speech aloud and put slash marks where you would normally pause.	X	
7. Refer to Chapter Four to review all of the elements for each communication style.	X	
8. Use flip charts with up to 50 audience members. For an audience of 100, select from among: large charts, slides or overhead transparencies.		X
9. Always be prepared to speak without visual accompaniment in the event that something should happen to your visual aids.		X
10. To insure clarity and continuity, one interest element is recommended.	X	
11. Intellects prefer to communicate with other Intellects. Nevertheless, care in selection of interest elements, etc. should be taken.	X	
12. First, try some of the other techniques suggested such as walking into your audience, asking questions, and establishing eye contact. If these don't work, then summarize and conclude.	X	
13. The type of clothing worn depends on your objective and the *type* of professional audience. Bob's audience consisted of professionals, yet they wore neutral clothing.		X

	TRUE	FALSE
14. When introducing a speaker, you are generally a known entity to the audience and your purpose is merely to set the stage for the speaker.	X	
15. In general, Passives have a large space requirement.		X
16. Rather than "I don't know," couple this response with an action statement, i.e. "I don't have that information right now; however, I will get it for you and give you a call."		X
17. Following your perspective you must also include a statement advising the audience of why the information is important to them.		X
18. Practice is always necessary because each audience is different and your information should be adapted to this audience.		X
19. Paralinguistics are signals that are received auditorily (in a form other than words) that contain meaning for the listener. Coughs, audible yawns, and silent pauses are examples.	X	
20. In order to gain rapport and involve your audience in your presentation, you should view it as a two-way exchange with your audience giving nonverbal feedback.	X	

REFERENCES

1. Barrett, Harold. *Practical Methods in Speech.* New York: Holt, Rinehart and Winston, 1977.
2. Burgoon, M., and Ruffner, M. *Human Communication.* New York: Holt, Rinehart and Winston, 1978.
3. Clevenger, Theodore, Jr. *Audience Analysis.* Indianapolis: Bobbs-Merrill Company, 1971.
4. Fujimoto, E. K. "The Comparative Power of Verbal and Non-verbal Symbols." Ph.D. dissertation, Ohio State University, 1971.
5. Gellerman, Saul W. *Motivation and Productivity.* New York: American Management Association, Inc., 1963.
6. Hill, W. F. *Learning: A Survey of Psychological Interpretation.* Scranton: Chandler Publishing Company, 1971.
7. Jung, C. E. *Collected Works of C. E. Jung.* Vol. 13. Princeton: Princeton University Press, 1967.
8. Kirkpatrick, D. *How to Plan and Conduct Productive Business Meetings.* Chicago: The Dartnell Corporation, 1976.
9. Knapp, M. *Nonverbal Communication in Human Interaction.* New York: Holt, Rinehart and Winston, 1978.
10. Malloy, J. *Dress for Success.* New York: Warner Books, 1976.
11. Malloy, J. *The Woman's Dress for Success.* Chicago: Follett Company, 1977.
12. McCabe, Bernard P. *Speaking is a Practical Matter.* Boston: Holbrook Press, 1968.
13. McCaskey, Michael B. The Hidden Messages Managers Send. *Harvard Business Review,* 57:135–148.
14. McClelland, David C., and Burnham, David H. "Power is the Great Motivator." *Harvard Business Review* 54:100–110.
15. McCroskey, J. C. *An Introduction to Rhetorical Communication.* Englewood Cliffs: Prentice-Hall, 1972.
16. McCroskey, J. C. *Measures of Communication-Bound Anxiety.* Speech Monographs Series, no. 37. Falls Church, VA: Speech Communication Association, 1970.
17. Miller, N., and Campbell, D. T. "Recency and Primacy in Persuasion as a Function of the Timing of Speeches and Measurements." *Journal of Abnormal and Social Psychology* 58:1–9.
18. Monroe, A. *Principles of Speech.* Glenview, IL: Scott Foresman and Company, 1958.
19. Monroe, A. H., and Ehninger, D. *Principles of Speech Communication.* 7th brief ed. Glenview, IL: Scott Foresman and Company, 1975.
20. Morris, D. *Manwatching.* New York: Harry N. Abrams, Inc., 1977.

21. Mortensen, D. *Communication: The Study of Human Interaction.* New York: McGraw-Hill Book Company, 1972.

22. Rogge, Edward, and Ching, James C. *Advanced Public Speaking.* New York: Holt, Rinehart and Winston, 1966.

23. Selye, H. *The Stress of Life.* New York: McGraw-Hill Book Company, 1976.

24. Smith, M. O. *Theoretical Foundations of Learning and Teaching.* Waltham, MA: Xerox College Publishing, 1971.

25. Visual Products Division, 3M Company. "Bright Ideas in Overhead Projections: A Guide to More Effective Meetings." St. Paul, MN: 3M Company, 1978.

26. Welke, J. W. "The Effects of Intensional and Extensional Audiences on Communicator Anxiety." *Central States Speech Journal* 19:14–18.

27. Young, J., and Mondy, R. *Personal Selling: Function, Theory and Practice.* Hinsdale, IL: The Dryden Press, 1978.

This is not the end!

Reinforce the techniques you've learned with a cassette tape! Continue to improve your presentation skills with authentic verbal examples to clarify the concepts covered in the text. Listen to pertinent sections just before you give a presentation; for example, review Chapter Three, "What About Nervousness," the morning before you speak. Have the convenience of learning any time—while you're driving to work, cooking dinner, or just relaxing!

Complete the program by ordering your *Winning Words* cassette today!

Yes, I'd like to improve my presentation skills with the *Winning Words* audio cassette tape (approximately 75 minutes). Please send me _____ cassette tape(s) at $13.95 each.

_____Payment enclosed (We pay postage and handling. Mass. residents add 5% sales tax.)

_____Charge to credit card (We pay postage and handling.)

_____Master Charge   _____VISA/BankAmericard   _____American Express

Account Number_____

Expiration Date_____

_____Bill me (You pay postage and handling. Authorized purchase order required on orders of $50.00 or more.)

Signature_____

(Signature required for processing of order.)

All foreign orders must be prepaid in U.S. dollars.

CBI Publishing Company, Inc.
51 Sleeper Street
Boston, Massachusetts   02210

(617) 426-2224